Poverty and development

INTRODUCTIONS TO SOCIOLOGY

Poverty and development

Johann Graaff

OXFORD
UNIVERSITY PRESS

OXFORD
UNIVERSITY PRESS

Great Clarendon Street, Oxford OX2 6DP

Oxford University Press is a department of the University of Oxford.
It furthers the University's objective of excellence in research, scholarship,
and education by publishing worldwide in

Oxford New York

Auckland Bangkok Buenos Aires Cape Town Chennai
Dar es Salaam Delhi Hong Kong Istanbul Karachi Kolkata
Kuala Lumpur Madrid Melbourne Mexico City Mumbai
Nairobi São Paulo Shanghai Taipei Tokyo Toronto

Oxford is a registered trade mark of Oxford University Press
in the UK and certain other countries

Published in South Africa
by Oxford University Press Southern Africa, Cape Town

Poverty and development
ISBN 0 19 578406 5

© Oxford University Press Southern Africa 2001

The moral rights of the author have been asserted
Database right Oxford University Press (maker)

First published 2003
Reprinted 2003

Commissioning editor: Arthur Attwell
Editor: Ken McGillivray
Indexer: John Linnegar
Designer: Kerry + Krynauw
Cover designer: Christopher Davis
Illustrators: Kerry + Krynauw

Published by Oxford University Press Southern Africa
PO Box 12119, N1 City, 7463, Cape Town, South Africa

Set in 9 pt on 12 pt ITC Garamond Light by Orchard Publishing
Reproduction by Castle Graphics
Cover reproduction by The Image Bureau
Printed and bound by Clyson Printers, Maitland, Cape Town

Contents

Introduction to the Series

This small book forms part of a series of small books. The series aims to present basic sociology in a somewhat different way. First, it presents foundational sociological topics in modular form, that is each topic is presented in a separate book. That gives them considerable flexibility. Topics can be variously combined to fit a wide spectrum of introductory courses. No longer will you need to buy a hugely expensive 400-page textbook of which you use only one quarter of the available chapters. With this series you can buy exactly what you want and use all of it. The first six topics will offer introductions to: sociology in general, population studies, social institutions (education and the family), poverty and development, work and organizations, and crime and deviance.

Secondly, each book is written in such a way that it tells a coherent story with a developing and cumulative theme. Too many textbooks are accumulations of vaguely related concepts containing no discernible thread or structure. Our view in this series is that logical and sequential argument is one of the prime skills students learn at university level. As such, the texts they work with must model that style, and the exercises they do must practise it. In consequence it is important not only that the style of writing be lucid, logical, and organized, but also that the exercises in the book be geared towards higher cognitive skills. You will see that the exercises at the end of each book are carefully constructed to test a range of thinking skills. At the same time, there is absolutely no reason why such discussions cannot be clear and accessible, written in language that flows and entertains as it educates. Annotated bibliographies can further this aim by indicating those existing sociological works which promote a similarly easy and rich style.

Thirdly, the various books deal with issues of some substance in sociology. They go beyond the elementary concepts which make up a particular problem area. They introduce students to debates that are current and alive in modern sociology. Clearly, an introductory textbook cannot expose its readers to the full complexity of technical argument. Texts therefore need to build up gradually a repertoire of technical language and an armoury of concepts, as is the case in any discipline. After all, you cannot simply get into a car and drive it without knowing how its controls, instruments, and signals work. But once you have the hang of it, it can become a thing of great power.

Fourthly, there are many sociology teachers who want sociology textbooks to be more accessible to southern African students, to use southern African examples, and promote something called 'southern African sociology'. While sociological writing in this subcontinent without doubt benefits from the use of southern African references and examples, and this series of books certainly pursues that practice, the spread of ethnic or cultural groups and ideological convictions, makes the existence of a southern African sociology, in the singular, very doubtful. Rather we would expect a range of sociologies, in the plural. But, even then, the influence of global sociological paradigms is so powerful that it is difficult to find anything which could be called distinctively 'southern African'. So, southern African reference points and examples, yes, but southern African sociology(ies) – very difficult.

Finally, sociology is a discipline that can reveal, open up, unveil the social world around us in wondrous ways. Its like cracking a secret code. It can make unthought-of, even unheard-of, connections and links. But it can also be personal and challenging. It can put question marks behind some of your most dearly held beliefs. Going on the sociological journey, then, can be exciting, surprising, angering, outrageous, and scary. It would not be true sociology if it were not.

Johann Graaff
Series Editor

Introduction

This book is about development, and development is about wealth and poverty in the world. Development is about why some people, and some countries, are rich, and others are poor, and how this wealth and this poverty are linked. Put differently, a central question in development studies is how some people's wealth is connected to other people's poverty. We could be very blunt and somewhat provocative, and also ask: whose fault is it that the Third World, in general, and Africa, in particular, are so poor today? Of course, causation is not the same as fault. The fact that you have inherited blue eyes from your parents does not necessarily mean that they are 'to blame' for your blue eyes. But it is in the nature of development studies that cause and blame often get entangled. (Should blame and cause go together in development, or not? What do you think?)

So, this book is primarily about causes. It is not primarily about blame. And causes entail theories. Theoretical language is causal language. It tells you how one thing causes another thing or, more frequently, how one set of circumstances produces another set of circumstances. But, like most social phenomena, development is a complex thing. Circumstances change with time and place. One country, or one region, is not the same as another. One historical period is not the same as another. This means that theories must change too. More importantly, people disagree about causes (often because they disagree about blame).

It follows that there are quite a lot of development theories. In order to make things clearer, we have arranged theories according to their origins either in functionalist theory, or in Marxist theory. We shall not say much about either functionalist theory or Marxist theory in themselves in this book because they are discussed in much more detail in the first book of this series, *What is Sociology?* (chapters 2 and 3). The plan of the book is sketched out overleaf. It shows the two broad streams of functionalist and Marxist theory. It also shows the start of the book, in chapter 1, with some basic definitions of poverty and development. Chapter 2 covers modernization theory and its development into the neo-liberalism of the World Bank, the International Monetary Fund (IMF), and the World Trade Organization (WTO). Chapter 3 covers Marxist theories of underdevelopment. The final chapter discusses Manuel Castells' important work and his thinking about informational capitalism. The diagram on the next page also shows one of the continuing themes in this book, namely globalization, and how it threads its way through all the chapters.

Development studies is about poverty and inequality within and between nations.

So much for the content. An important aspect of this book (and indeed of this whole series of books) is its attempt to present a coherent argument, a sequence of steps which follow from the start of the book to its end, that is, a continuing theme. Over the last 50 years development studies has embodied many continuing themes. In this book we have chosen to highlight four main themes.

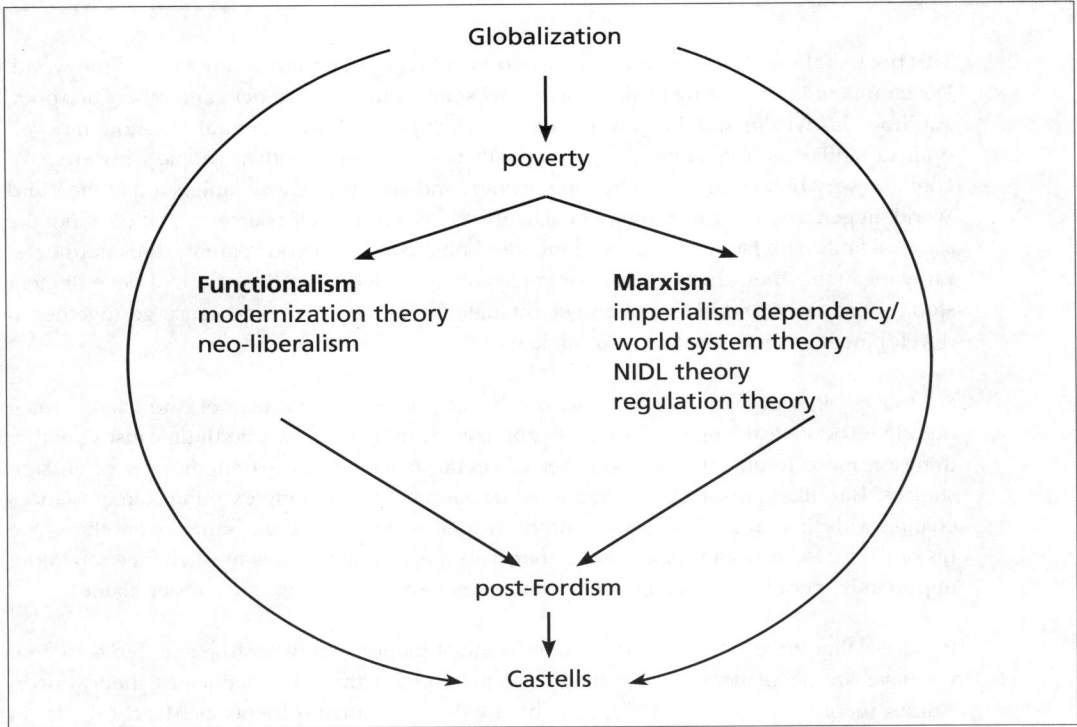

Globalization

↓

poverty

Functionalism
modernization theory
neo-liberalism

Marxism
imperialism dependency/
world system theory
NIDL theory
regulation theory

post-Fordism

↓

Castells

Fig: Broad strands of development theory covered in this book

The first of these is the way in which development theories of both the modernization and neo-Marxist varieties have grappled with the phenomenon of *extremely rapid development in the Far East*. Neo-Marxist theories, in particular, have struggled to understand what was happening in the East Asian 'tigers'.

A second theme that flows through many parts of this book is the *process of gradual sophistication in neo-Marxist theories*. Given their roots in 'orthodox' Marxism, these theories have all downplayed the role of the state and culture in development. They have focused far too much attention on economics. Over time this has changed, and later theories, such as regulation theory, have been much more flexible and inclusive.

A third central theme has been that of *globalization*. Early modernization theory simply ignored the influence of colonial conquest, for example, on Third World societies. Neo-Marxist theories, in contrast, have from the outset recognized the critical importance of globalization, but often in simplistic ways. Manuel Castells' vision of a global information society brings this particular sequence to an end.

A fourth theme running through this book is *the conversation between theories*. This book introduces you to the basic principles of a wide range of theories. But the introduction is of a critical kind. Each theory is subjected to comment and criticism, often on the part of other theories. It is an important principle of development theory − indeed, of all social science theory − that theories move all the time. They respond to new circumstances, they point out faults in earlier theories, they attempt to make improvements in their own analyses.

But that is not a random process. It is not the case that we have dozens of voices all babbling away, just making noise. As you read you will perceive a cumulative learning happening. There may be many voices speaking (and that in itself certainly makes for interesting reading), but those voices do hear one another, they do learn. Development theory of the 1990s and the 2000s is immensely more sophisticated than it was in the 1960s. The conversation in the intervening 50 years shows us how we got there.

1 Poverty and Development

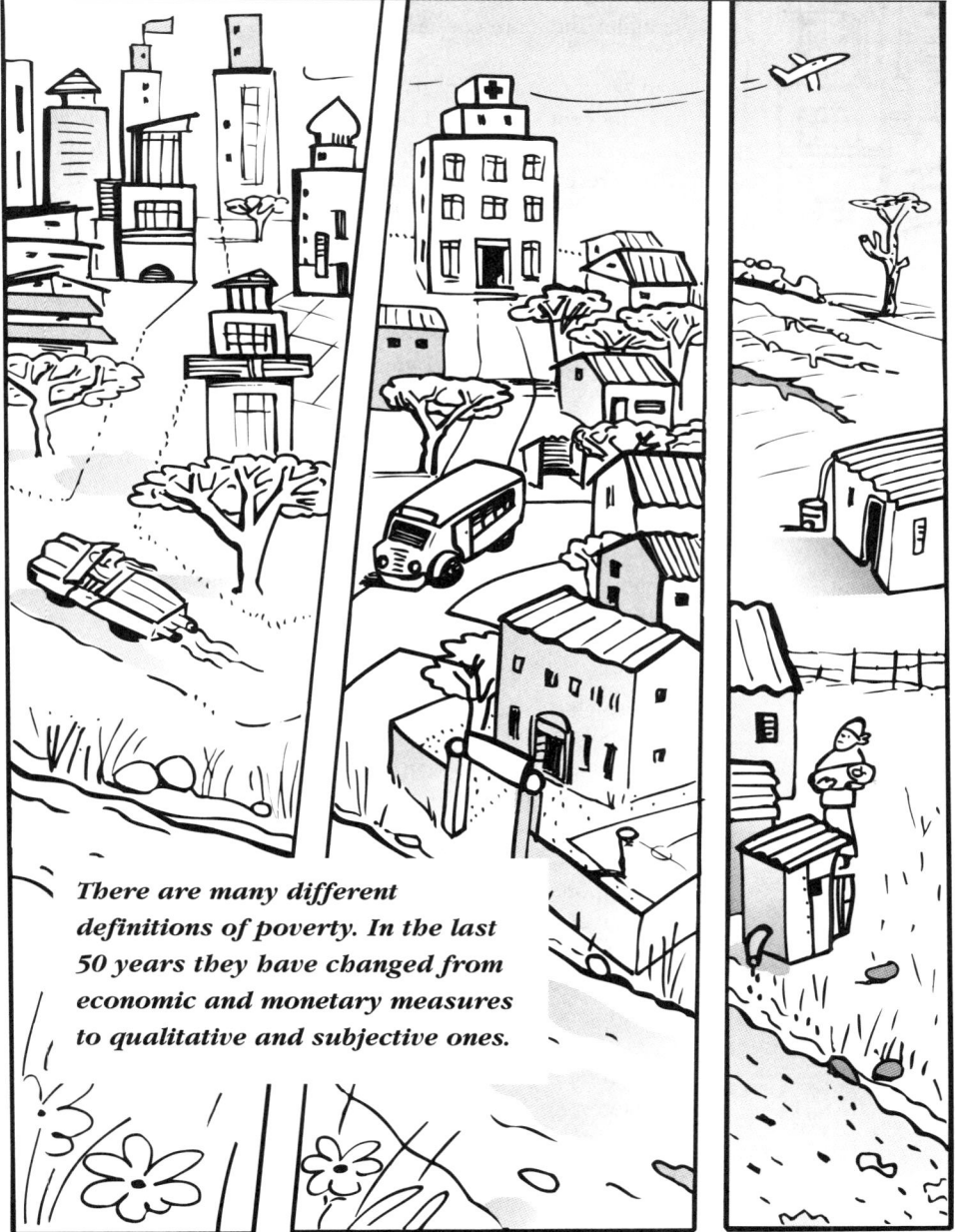

There are many different definitions of poverty. In the last 50 years they have changed from economic and monetary measures to qualitative and subjective ones.

Introduction

Our task in this chapter is to provide workable definitions for some of the concepts at the foundation of this book, namely 'development', 'poverty', 'inequality', 'Third World', and 'First World'. We shall see that, like many other concepts, they are fairly simple at first glance, but that they become more complex the more you investigate their detail.

Part of that complexity has to do with the fact that defining concepts is not an innocent exercise. Concepts reflect theoretical concerns and ideological conflicts. And so it is with concepts such as development and poverty. They are expressions, containers, of almost 50 years of debate and politics. Definitions have their defenders and their critics. Their general acceptance is a sign of the power of those who propose them. The term 'Third World' for example, is a reflection of the now long gone Cold War. So the First World comprised Europe, America, Japan, Australia, and New Zealand. The Second World comprised the communist bloc. And the Third World comprised the 'new' nations of Africa, Latin America, and Asia.

Poverty, development and inequality are at the heart of development studies – for two reasons. The first is that development studies concerns itself for the largest part with the nature and origins of poverty and inequality, both within individual countries and also across many countries. Development studies seeks to understand the causes of these phenomena, to construct theories about their origins, and from there to formulate practical policies for alleviating those conditions.

Secondly, and more importantly, development studies is, above all else, a moral enterprise. It is about compassion for, and empathy with, those who are less fortunate than ourselves, for those who struggle to survive. This is a sentiment which runs deep in most of the world's cultures and religions. It is not difficult to find injunctions in holy books the world over to seek out, to nurture, to assist, 'the poor'.

It is important to know that we are not just studying the poverty of individuals but also that of countries. And in the writing about these topics, the term 'poverty' often refers mostly to individuals, whereas the term 'development' refers to countries. You find underdeveloped or less developed countries, but not underdeveloped or less developed individuals.

So development studies, poverty, and inequality are all linked to one another in interesting and complex ways. In the rest of this chapter we examine the various ways of measuring poverty and inequality. We shall see how complicated a phenomenon it is.

Measures of development and poverty

There has been an important change in the measurement of development and poverty since the first Development Decade (1960–1970). At that time social scientists were content to use mostly economic measures. The development of countries, and their annual growth, was measured by *gross national product* (GNP). The poverty of people was measured by the basic amount of money necessary to keep someone alive. And the two concepts were linked. Higher rates of GNP growth meant lower levels of poverty. But both poverty and development were economic concepts.

It soon became evident, however, that in many countries GNP was growing at a satisfactory rate but poverty was worsening. Healthy economic growth was no guarantee against widening inequality. South Africa is a case in point. It grew at quite spectacular rates during the 1950s and 1960s, but it produced one of the most extreme cases of inequality in the world.

Two things changed. First, alongside GNP as a measure, came measures of inequality in the population. So, for example, social scientists began to measure how the income of the top 10 per cent of the population compared with that of the bottom 40 per cent. Secondly, alongside economic measures came measures of educational level, physical health, and political democracy. They began to realize that poverty is as much about quality of life, power, and access to resources as about income.

So, let us start by considering the measurement of absolute poverty, that is, what it takes to keep someone alive.

Absolute poverty

Perhaps the most basic measures of poverty in South Africa are the *Minimum Living Level* (MLL) (as published each year by the Bureau of Market Research (BMR)) and the *Household Subsistence Level* (HSL) (as measured by the University of Port Elizabeth) (Wilson & Ramphele 1989). They measure the amount of money necessary to provide a household (of six people) with the very elementary necessities to stay alive. Those basic necessities include food, clothing, fuel or lighting, washing, rent, and transport. The World Bank's similar *poverty line* includes 'the necessary expenditure to buy the minimum standard of nutrition and other necessities' (May 2000: 29).

In South Africa in 1999 the MLL for an individual was R164,20 per month. That amounts to approximately R5,30 per day. (Do you think you could cook, eat, clothe, and warm yourself on R5,30 a day? Imagine what you would need to do in order to achieve that.) The poverty line for a household was R353 per month

in the same year. On the basis of these figures Taylor calculated that 18 million people in South Africa lived below the poverty line in 1999 (Taylor 2000: 55).

But the MLL is an extremely basic measure. It covers very little in the average life of an individual or a family. For these reasons the BMR now publishes an annual Household Effective Level (HEL), which is the HSL plus 50 per cent. It is intended to cover some important items not covered by the HSL, namely tax, medical expenses, replacement of household equipment, education, recreation/entertainment, personal care, pension, UIF, and burial contributions. In 1999 for South Africa that would have amounted to R799,50 per month. The average wage for unskilled workers in mining in South Africa was R770 a month in 1996 (May 2000: 77).

Relative deprivation and structural poverty

One of the serious problems with measures of absolute poverty is that they do not take into account the expectations, norms, values, and customs of particular communities in which people live. While individuals may be able to stay alive on a certain income, they might feel profoundly disadvantaged within particular local situations. If an individual is unable to participate in the normal routines of his or her community, he or she would experience a poverty of life which might be equally as painful as physical deprivation. So, for example, someone might not be able to send their children to school in a country where the law requires one to do so.

For these reasons social scientists now distinguish absolute poverty from relative poverty or *relative deprivation*. Measures of relative deprivation consider people's perception of how poor they feel. Significantly they are measures which recognize some of the complexity of poverty. They recognize that poverty is not just a physical phenomenon.

Being poor is not just being without money. Being poor frequently also means being subjected to physical abuse and violence, being subjected to humiliation and indignity, being subjected to exploitation by the powerful and the wealthy. It frequently involves experiences of humiliation, of helplessness, of ill health, of indignity, of anxiety, of rejection and denigration, of powerlessness and insecurity, of fatalism, of being trapped in a terribly bleak place, and of deep injustice.

Over 50 years the calculation of poverty has changed from simpler economic measures to more complex qualitative ones.

In other words, poverty is not a simple phenomenon. It has economic, political, cultural, emotional, and psychological dimensions. It means that people suffer many more wounds than just the physical, and it means that poverty is a state of vulnerability. Physical deprivation, then, is often a symptom of something more important, namely, a position of structural deprivation, an exposure to exploitation and abuse which people are unable to escape (Webster 1990).

For these reasons, also, newer studies of poverty have conducted detailed interviews with poor people. They have wanted to convey the 'feel' of poverty, the subjective experience of it. It is not possible to understand, especially, relative deprivation without understanding how individuals concretely experience being poor, how they themselves define poverty (May 2000: 41).

> *Poverty is not knowing where your next meal is to come from, and always wondering when the council is going to put your furniture out and always praying that your husband must not lose his job. To me that is poverty* (Mrs Witbooi, quoted in Wilson & Ramphele 1989: 14).

Here we can see the effect of changing theoretical analyses of poverty. There was a time when poverty was seen as a symptom of laziness, of personal irresponsibility, of individuals who simply lacked moral fibre, or of traditional superstition. People were solely and individually responsible for their own fortunes (Webster 1990). (You will recognize this later as *modernization theory*.)

Later analyses of poverty recognize that people are often the victims of situations which they cannot influence. These analyses acknowledge that poverty may be the result of a whole pattern of interlocking factors and that removing only one of them may do very little to solve the problem (Webster 1990).

Later still, analyses of poverty have taken into account the personal experience and the subjective side of poverty. They have recognized that poverty cannot be understood solely in cold figures and clinical causal factors. There is an important qualitative side to poverty.

The point to underline here is that the 'simple' notions of poverty and development can be, and usually are, incorporated into much larger theoretical patterns.

Fig 1.1: Changing definitions of poverty

Economic	Absolute poverty, GDP per capita
Subjective, cultural	Relative deprivation
Qualitative, inequality	Human Development Index
Sociological	Structural deprivation

Let us now turn from the consideration of individual poverty to national development.

Measuring development

As indicated above, the first criterion which people used to compare countries was *gross national product* (GNP). GNP is the total value of all the goods and services produced in a country in a particular year. When you divide that total by the number of people in a country, you get *per capita* GNP. That is still today seen as an easy and quick way to compare the relative wealth of various countries. So, in 1997, Switzerland, the country with the highest per capita income in the world (US$44 320) was 114 times richer than India (US$390) and 403 times richer than Ethiopia (US$110) (Todaro 2000: 44).

The World Bank takes the 133 countries of the world whose populations are more than a million, and divides them into four categories according to their per capita GNP. These are:

- *low-income countries* (with per capita GNP less than US$785 in 1997);
- *middle income* (between US$786 and US$3 125);
- *upper middle income* (between US$3 126 and US$9 655), and
- *high income* (above US$9 655).

There are 26 countries that fall into the high-income bracket, and 107 which fall into the remaining three categories (Todaro 2000: 30).

But this is a hugely problematic way of comparing countries and of measuring development. Most importantly, per capital GNP says nothing about how wealth is spread between different sections of the population. That is, it hides levels of inequality in a country.

In 1990 the United Nations Development Programme (UNDP) proposed a Human Development Index (HDI) to counter some of these problems. As a value the HDI ranges between 0 and 1. The HDI measures more than just income. It also includes life expectancy and educational attainment. And while these three indices are fragmentary and seemingly arbitrary measures of poverty and of basic quality of life, they are intended as proxies for a wider range of aspects. That means that they measure more than one specific aspect. Life expectancy, for example, indicates not only how long people are expected to live, but also something about their state of health at both physical and emotional levels. Educational attainment, likewise, measures not only the effectiveness of the schooling system but also people's skill levels and their chances of employment. Where the HDI does measure income, it does not do so in monetary terms but as adjusted against the local cost of living (Taylor 2000: 219).

What does South Africa look like in terms of the HDI? The first point to make is that, although South Africa (at US$3 040 per capita GNP) ranks alongside a country such as Malaysia (US$3 480), on the HDI it ranks with countries such as Paraguay and Botswana. In other words, South Africa's HDI ranking is a whole lot worse than its per capita GNP ranking.

The second point is that the various provinces and the various races of South Africa show sharply different levels. Among the provinces, Gauteng ranks first (along with countries such as Singapore and Venezuela), while Limpopo ranks last (alongside countries such as Namibia and Lesotho). The same applies to the racial ranking among whites, Indians, coloureds, and Africans. The fact that Limpopo is the most rural of all the provinces, tells us something about the dramatic gap between urban and rural areas in South Africa (May 2000: 24).

As with our measures of poverty, HDI indices have an underlying theory of development which is different from GNP-based measures. Those earlier measurements were strongly economically based, and worked from the assumption that development was mainly an economic phenomenon. Later indices such as the HDI have a different theory of development. Here development is a multi-faceted phenomenon with significant roots in structural inequalities and power differences. We shall see as we go further that there is a third broad conception of development which relates to the structural relationship between countries. These theories, of which the best known is *dependency theory*, do not speak of a lack of development, but rather of 'active underdevelopment'.

Why is inequality so important? Why do so many social scientists place emphasis on it these days? After all, there are many who may be 'less fortunate' but nevertheless can lead perfectly comfortable, healthy lives.

There are a number of reasons why they worry about them, and why they are right to worry about them. The first is again a moral reason. There is something fundamentally wrong with a planet which has the resources to send a rocket to Venus, but where more than a billion individuals survive on US$1 a day.

The second reason is a political one. A country where there is a high level of inequality is very vulnerable to political instability. Economic inequality often translates into political resentment, unrest, and conflict. A country with a high level of inequality is not likely to be a peaceful place to live.

The third reason is economic. There are serious arguments for believing that a country's economic growth will be significantly inhibited if large parts of its citizenry are illiterate, unskilled, politically angry, and unsupported by the government in their attempts to make a living. Economic growth, therefore, cannot just be for a minority in a country. For the country to prosper, it must utilize its whole population and use the full range of potential at its disposal.

Definitions of poverty reflect a background of ideological and political struggles.

Conclusion

In this chapter we have investigated various notions of poverty, development, and inequality. We have seen that definitions and measures such as these are not merely statistical figures. They reflect ideological and theoretical commitments which have built up over the past 50 years. Thus, earlier income-based measures such as the various poverty lines, and per capita GNP assumed a view of development which placed responsibility on individual people and their values. Later measures see poverty and development as much more complex where politics, psychology, sociology, and culture play significant roles. Inequality between the top and bottom layers of society, between the rich and the poor, are now seen as problematic aspects which obstruct development and waste a country's resources.

In the chapters which follow we begin to investigate in more detail how various theories of development work.

2 Modernization Theory

In modernization theory, Third World countries are expected to catch up with First World countries culturally, politically, and economically. In terms of this theory, they need to break out of the 'shackles of tradition' to become modern.

Introduction

In chapter 1 we examined the nature and the measurement of poverty. In this chapter we start out on the business of explaining the origins of poverty, how it is caused and, consequently, how one can solve it. As we indicated earlier, there are two currents of such explanation (that is of theory) in understanding what causes poverty. One derives from functionalism, and the other from Marxism. In this chapter we commence with an investigation of the functionalist stream.

Modernization theory arose in the United States in the period after World War II. During the 1950s and 1960s it enjoyed immense popularity in First World countries. It was a quite explicit attempt to construct a justification for the Western, capitalist way of life in its competition with communism during the time of the Cold War. It was a time when the old colonial empires built by a number of European powers, in particular Britain, were fragmenting. New nations were becoming politically independent. It was very important for the West that these countries not fall under the influence of the Soviet Union. The battle for the 'hearts and minds' of Third World countries was conducted in military, political, financial, diplomatic, and economic arenas. Modernization theory was the intellectual and academic leg of this strategy (So 1990: 17).

Modernization theory was not a neat theory. It spread itself, almost sprawled, across a variety of disciplines – politics, sociology, economics, psychology, anthropology. And we should not expect it to be neat. Any vibrant theoretical current will sprout a great number of branches. Some of these might clash with others. For the sake of simplicity we shall examine here only three areas of the theory, namely *evolutionism, functionalism,* and *neo-liberalist* economics.

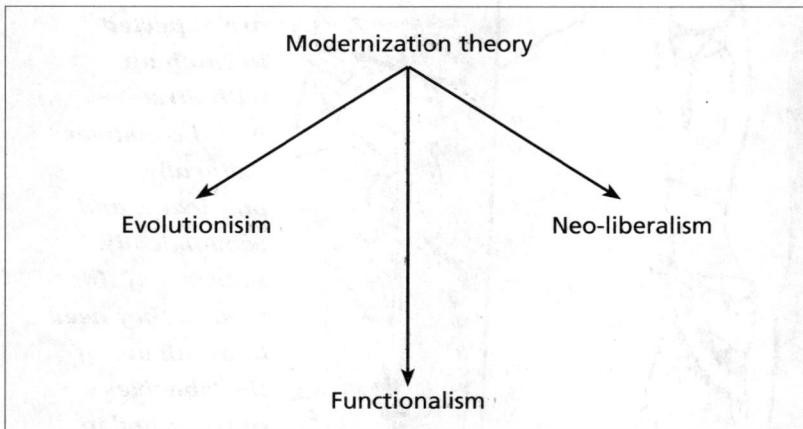

Fig 2.1: Three areas of modernization theory

By the beginning of the twenty-first century, large parts of modernization theory had been completely demolished – which is why we are writing about it in the past tense. Both the evolutionist and functionalist aspects of modernization theory have virtually disappeared from development studies – and we will see why. Neo-classical economics, however, has survived, in somewhat changed form, as neo-liberalism. During the 1980s this was the policy very powerfully propagated by Prime Minister Margaret Thatcher of Great Britain, and President Ronald Reagan of the United States. Their support of neo-liberal economics was also taken up by the International Monetary Fund (IMF) and the World Bank, and taken through well into the 1990s. As I write, this policy still has strong support around the world, but resistance to it in the form of anti-globalization protest and in academic critique has spread immensely. We shall have to wait and see what happens to it.

The shackles of tradition

What did modernization theory say? In a nutshell, it suggested to Third World countries that, in order to progress economically, politically, and socially, they should follow the example of what First World countries had done. 'Do what we did, and become like us' was the message. Politically that meant democratically elected government and a free press; economically it meant a capitalist economy, industrialization, urbanization, and the commercialization of subsistence agriculture; socially it meant the spread of educational and health services; and culturally it meant the adoption of modern individualist and rational values. And the greatest obstacle to all of these was 'the shackles of tradition', that is, traditional values which placed religion and family above efficiency and the market, and which blocked progress with fatalism and backward-looking conservatism.

Modernization theory tells the Third World to follow the ways of the First World.

We need to distinguish here between the two terms 'modernization' and 'modernism'. They may look pretty similar, but I am going to use them in slightly different ways. Modernism or modernity refers to the condition of being modern, and the various political, cultural, social, or economic aspects of that. Modernization, in contrast, refers to the process by which Third World countries catch up with First World countries, the process by which these 'new' nations try to replicate in the twentieth century what the 'old' ones did in the eighteenth and nineteenth centuries. Modernization theory, then, is one way to explain how that happens.

Let us now consider the three legs of modernization theory in more detail.

Darwin's legacy: evolutionism

As the name suggests, evolutionism has its roots in the biological writings of Charles Darwin, whose book, *On the Origin of Species*, published in 1859, caused such a stir in England and Europe. Darwin argued that, contrary to biblical teaching, animals and humans had not been created, fully formed, and placed by divine will on the Earth. Rather they had descended, evolved, through millions of years, from earlier and simpler forms of life. Human beings were the culmination of this process, the highest and most advanced form of life on Earth.

The classical sociologists of the nineteenth century were profoundly influenced by Darwin's form of argument. Writers such as Durkheim, Marx, Tönnies, Weber, and Spencer all argued that modern societies had evolved gradually through a series of earlier and more 'primitive' stages. Like human beings, modern societies were the highest and most advanced forms of society on Earth. The term 'modern societies' of course meant Europe and the West. What we today call the 'Third World' (Africa, Latin America, Asia) were, for social evolutionists, several rungs further down on the ladder of progress (So 1990: 19; Webster 1990: 41–62).

It seemed a compelling and almost self-evident scheme. The simplest and most primitive societies were the *hunter-gatherers*, such as the forest pygmies or the southern African San. The next stage up were the *pastoralists* who farmed with plants and animals. Then came the *ancient empires*, the Egyptians, the Romans, and the Greeks, with considerably more complex forms of technology, government, and social organization. This phase was followed by *feudalism*, which saw the birth of the printing press and the spread of literacy, and the immense structure of the Roman Catholic Church. And finally, *capitalist industrial* society, the most advanced on all levels – technologically, politically, administratively, economically, socially, and culturally. Any society positioned further down the ladder, these writers maintained, would have to traverse all the subsequent stages to reach modernity.

The fundamental principles of evolutionist thinking, then, can be spelled out as follows (So 1990: 34–5; Webster 1990: 41–62). Among human societies, social change:

- occurs gradually and over a long period of time; it is evolutionary, not revolutionary;
- goes through a set number of stages; and all societies go through the same stages;
- is irreversible; change goes 'forward' only;
- is progressive; later societies are superior to earlier ones, and
- converges to a single form; all societies end up looking the same.

We shall see further on that each of these principles has been the subject of thoroughgoing critique. None of them has survived intact. Despite that stringent critique, however, a new form of evolutionary thinking has arisen which is more viable, but it has jettisoned all its original biological assumptions.

During the nineteenth and early twentieth centuries Darwin's thinking, as we have indicated, enjoyed immense popularity, particularly among the classical sociologists. However, there was a more ominous stream of thinking which also grew out of biological Darwinism known as social Darwinism. It followed the notion that evolution proceeded in the basis of the principle of the 'survival of the fittest'. Social Darwinists came to the dangerous conclusion that those who survived, that is those who were the strongest, were also morally and culturally superior. In certain quarters that was translated into racial (and racist) terms to say that the European white (Caucasian) races were superior to other races. We shall see that this principle of moral superiority remained part of evolutionist thinking.

In the next sections I examine two examples of evolutionist writers. These are Talcott Parsons and Walt Rostow. Parsons was probably the most eminent American sociologist of the late twentieth century. During the 1950s and 1960s he so dominated sociology that Parsonian structural functionalism was seen almost as synonymous with sociology. Sociologists used to joke that when you studied sociology you studied Parsons. Although he did not write much on development, many development writers drew heavily on his work, particularly his writing on evolution. Parsons' work focused quite strongly on modernism rather than modernization. It covered a much longer stretch of time in human history and had no prescriptions on how development should happen.

Walt Rostow, in contrast, was an economist. His most famous book, *The Stages of Economic Growth*, significantly, was sub-titled *A Non-Communist Manifesto* (Rostow 1960). This book covered a much shorter period of time, and had clear suggestions on how newly developing and industrializing countries should plan their economic growth. It was, in other words, a clear example of *modernization* rather than *modernist writing*.

Overall, Parsons is a more sophisticated writer than Rostow. We shall see that Rostow tried to formulate a model for development in Third World countries. That attempt failed. I shall argue that all such attempts must fail because they do not take into account the multitude of differences between countries, nor the fact that individuals reflect on their own histories.

Parsons and evolutionary universals

Let us start, then, with Parsons. On the face of it Parsons has a quite simple historical scheme for the evolution of human society through a series of stages (see figure 2.1 below). In this scheme there are four stages through which human societies have moved before reaching the modern stage, exemplified by the United States.

Fig 2.2: Parsons' historical scheme

Societal type	Example
Primitive	Australian Aborigines
Advanced primitive	Nineteenth-century Zulus
Intermediate	Ancient Egypt
Advanced intermediate	Imperial Rome, China
Modern	United States

There are two aspects of Parsons' thinking, however, which make it more than just a simple scheme. The first is his notion of an *evolutionary universal*. This is an attribute of society which is essential for it to move 'up' to the next stage. Writing is such an evolutionary universal. Without writing, the administrative capacity of any society is sharply limited. No state, for example, would be able to gather taxes in any efficient way without having an efficient system of records. There is, in fact, evidence that the first forms of writing were used precisely for the purposes of tax collection (Giddens 1984; Parsons 1966).

Evolutionary universals are societal attributes which have very frequently been discovered independently in a number of different societies. Language, writing, and religion are such essential elements which have all arisen in their different forms quite separately in numerous societies over time.

Thinking about evolution in this way makes things slightly more interesting because it means that there is no single path which societies must follow. They can discover and combine various evolutionary universals in various ways and at different times. Certain steps, though, such as state tax collection, will be denied them if they have not put in place particular evolutionary universals.

The other interesting thing about Parsons is that he is not proposing a *theory* of evolution. The various stages of evolution were, for Parsons, rather categorizations of societal types. He was not offering any *explanation* of how they moved from one stage to the next (Parsons 1966: 11). That makes it very difficult to offer any formula for newly modernizing societies. (Subsequent writers have frequently ignored these subtleties in Parsons' writing.)

If we measure Parsons against the five principles of typical evolutionist writing, he conforms to only three of them. For Parsons:

- Social change is gradual and not revolutionary.
- It is progressive in the sense that later societies (and particularly the United States) are seen as superior to earlier ones.
- Societies do tend to look the same as they develop.
- He does not believe, however, in a set number of stages that all societies have to go through in the same order, that is, there is not a model of change which societies will follow nor is there an explanation of why they shift from one stage to another.
- Change is not irreversible. He does acknowledge that change can be 'backward' in some cases.

Other writers have not been so reticent. The best known classical writers who did this were Durkheim and Marx. We shall see that Rostow also has a causal explanation of how one stage shifts to another. It is critical for writers who are proposing a generalizable model that there be a causal sequence that they can point to.

Rostow's evolutionary scheme

Like Parsons, Rostow also has five stages in his historical scheme. However, that is just about the only way in which they are similar. In all other aspects Rostow is different from Parsons. Rostow's second stage, preconditions for take-off, describes the beginnings of capitalism. In other words, he does not consider hunter-gatherer, pastoralist, or feudal societies as worth describing separately. They all fit neatly into his term 'traditional society'.

The second thing to note about his scheme is that he considers it to be both explanatory and a model for newer countries who wish to hasten their own development. Of his five stages Rostow says:

These stages are not merely descriptive. They are not merely a way of generalizing certain factual observations about the sequence of development of modern societies. They have an inner logic. They have an analytic bone-structure, rooted in a dynamic theory of production. ... They constitute, in the end, ... a theory about economic growth ... (Rostow 1960: 12–13).

Fig 2.3: Rostow's stages of development

Stage	Significant characteristics
1 Traditional society	1 Pre-Newtonian science, limited production, fatalism
2 Preconditions for take-off	2 New attitude to change, expanding population, entrepreneurial class
3 Take-off	3 Development of science, discovery of new continents, nationalist spirit, national savings of 10 per cent
4 Drive to maturity	4 Economic growth becomes normal, differentiated industrialization
5 The age of high mass-consumption	5 Pursuit of external power, welfare state, mass consumption

We do not need to follow the finer detail of Rostow's scheme, but there are three key points worth remembering. First, a critical moment in the change from traditional society is the shift from a fatalistic attitude to one where progress and change are seen as normal. Fatalism implies an attitude in which 'the range of possibilities open to one's grandchildren would be just about what it had been for one grandparents' (Rostow 1960: 5). Although this represents a significant shift in society, economic growth will not take off while there is high population growth which soaks up whatever surplus is produced.

As an evolutionist, Parsons is much more sophisticated than Rostow.

The second critical moment for Rostow, then, is some stimulus which jolts the economy, something like a political revolution, the spread of a nationalist spirit, or a new technological discovery. This helps to push a country into its take-off stage.

The third and most important critical moment is when national savings and investment rise to 10 per cent of national income. This is the factor that pushes a country into self-sustained growth. Importantly, this factor, says Rostow, can be supplemented by external aid. For countries of the West, entangled as they were in the Cold War, that was a most helpful suggestion (So 1990: 17). We shall see later that this trust in the effect of rising investment was an important part of the commitment to free market capitalism in the post-war period (Todaro 2000).

In the South African context, Rostow's ideas were taken up with some enthusiasm. Economists such as Hobart Houghton and Michael O'Dowd used Rostow's ideas not only to analyse South African history, but also, remarkably in O'Dowd's case, to predict when social change would occur.

> *About 1980, one can look for the radical constitutional reform, corresponding to the Second Reform Act in England ... the final stage, the era of the welfare state, should be reached by about the turn of the century* (O'Dowd 1996: 116).

Evolutionist thinking, whether of the Rostow or any other variety, has not lasted. It is too shot through with problems. Let us examine what these problems are.

What's wrong with evolutionism?

I have already hinted at a number of criticisms of evolutionist thinking. Let me spell these out. The first and most important is that it often displays a level of Eurocentric arrogance in assuming that the highest point of human history is represented by European countries and the United States. We saw also how one leg of that moral stance developed into quite racist versions of social Darwinism. Both Parsons and Rostow are guilty of this kind of moral arrogance (Giddens 1984: 273–4).

The second problem with evolutionist thinking is its attempt to provide a model of growth which other countries can follow. There are two important reasons why this is wrong. The first is to assume that the history of one country can be transposed on to another. This is often done by taking an (economic) slice out of a particular country's history while ignoring its political, cultural and social aspects. That makes for extremely unrealistic comparisons. The second reason is that people can and do reflect on their own conditions and those of other countries. They draw (sound or unsound) lessons from that reflection and try to do things differently. In other words, people's attitudes to their past changes, and that changes a critical part of how history happens. In an important sense, then, history cannot repeat itself because the people living that history are not the same as they were (Giddens 1984: 273–4). Here it is Rostow rather than Parsons who is the guilty one.

Thirdly, evolutionist thinking is globally naïve thinking. It tends to assume that changes in a society are internally generated, independent of the influence of other societies. As we shall see in the next chapter, any one society's development is almost always shaped, pushed, and distorted by its contact with other more powerful or less powerful societies. In a global system countries form part of wider patterns which include dozens of other countries. To be

Evolutionism is the weakest of the three legs of modernization theory.

anywhere near realistic, evolutionists would have to think of an evolution of those patterns of countries, but certainly not of single countries.

So far in our critique we have concentrated on the notions that social change:
- is progressive, making later societies superior to earlier ones, and
- that it goes through a set number of stages, and can be repeatable.

The remainder of the five evolutionist principles that we started out with can be dealt with much more quickly. The evolutionist notion that social change is gradual and happens over a long period of time ignores the frequency of social and political revolutions throughout human history, and the equally wrenching experience of military conquest. None of these can be classified as slow and peaceful.

The principle that all societies converge to a single form is, of course, a matter of definition. To say that all industrialized societies are similar depends on how much one concentrates on technology and how much one ignores linguistic, cultural, religious, and political aspects.

That leaves only the final principle, namely that social change is irreversible, that it always goes 'forwards'. This principle also flies in the face of even quite recent evidence. We have seen countries such as Argentina collapse economically. We have seen countries such as Mozambique and Angola collapse both economically and politically. We have seen countries such as Afghanistan reject cultural modernity and revert quite forcibly to traditional norms and institutions.

However, before we throw out also this principle of evolutionist thinking, let us remember Parsons' idea of evolutionary universals. There is something compelling about the idea that societies cannot move 'up' in the evolutionary hierarchy until they put in place certain essential building blocks. Let us put this differently, in terms of individuals rather than societies. In Parsonian terms, individual members of society would find it difficult to give up the advantages of certain institutional arrangements, technological discoveries or organizational practices. Would people who have learnt to write wish to revert to illiteracy? Would people who had discovered the administrative and political advantages of the nation-state want to revert to a stateless localized existence? Especially in a world of global competition? Of course, nothing is inconceivable, and so it is possible that there may be people who will take these decisions. But it seems very unlikely.

It is on this basis that some writers today are arguing that social changes might not be completely irreversible, but that they might be 'sticky downward'. Once it has reached a certain level, it is highly unlikely that social change will move 'down' again (Hallpike 1986; Wright et al 1992: 79).

In summary, then, we have seen that the five principles of evolutionist thinking, that social change happens *gradually*; *in repeatable stages*; *irreversibly*; *forward*, and *towards a single end form* have all been subjected to drastic critique. The only one that survives in any form is *the third*, that social change tends to keep going in a particular direction. But we can only do that if we reject biological Darwinian argument and use something like Parsons' evolutionary universals.

We now move to consider the second of the three legs of modernization theory, namely, functionalism. In this we can be somewhat briefer.

Parts and wholes: functionalism

In the first book of this series we examined both Parsons' and Durkheim's functionalism in some detail. In summary, functionalism has that name since it analyses the positive benefits (the functions) which parts of society bring to the whole. Each part has a particular contribution to make in the maintenance and continued existence of the bigger entity. For Parsons, there are four subsystems in society: the economic, the political, the cultural, and the social. Each of these specific areas brings a broad benefit to society (Graaff 2001). For our purposes, what is important is that the cultural subsystem is the ultimate guarantor of social cohesion. What holds society together are the basic values and norms which people hold in common. These basic values are often lodged in religion, but this is not always the case.

Values, and the general consensus which people have around values, are what anchor society. It is values which hold all the other parts, all the other subsystems, in place. Earlier we wrote of the 'shackles of tradition' which hold traditional societies back from development. Tradition and custom operate in the area of values. In other words, tradition and custom are at the very centre of a society's stability. If tradition and custom change, then a great many other things will change. If they do not change, it will be very difficult to change other parts of society.

What would it look like if we translated a broad society's values into relationships between individual people? This is the point of Parsons' pattern variables. These describe the different relationships which would prevail in either traditional or modern societies.

Parsons' pattern variables

Alongside his writings on evolution, the second element in Parsons' writing which has been frequently used in development thinking, is his *pattern variables*. Whereas Parsons used this idea for a range of other purposes, later writers have used them as a way to distinguish social relations in modern societies from those in earlier ones.

You will recognize here the characteristics of two sharply different kinds of society. One is a small-scale, stable, traditional (village) society where people often know one another and relate on a face-to-face, trusting, and personal basis. People treat one another as they would family members. Much effort goes into maintaining harmony in the group. The other is a modern, rapidly shifting, urban society in which people typically have to deal with strangers. Their relationships are often impersonal, formal, and detached. In relationships harmony is often sacrificed for efficiency and profit.

The figure below lists these pattern variables as five pairs of attributes.

Fig 2.4: Parsons' pattern variables

Pre-modern	Modern
1 Affective	Affective-neutral
2 Particularistic	Universalistic
3 Collective orientation	Self-orientation
4 Ascription	Achievement
5 Functionally diffuse	Functionally specific

Let us consider these briefly (So 1990). The first item on the table refers to the emotional content in interaction. In small-scale traditional societies the contact between individuals is emotionally coloured. They treat one another as family members. In modern society people typically treat one another in an impersonal way as strangers.

The second item in the list refers also to criteria for interaction between people, where individuals are judged by broad universal standards (as citizens) or by particularities (such as race, gender, sexual orientation).

The third item refers to the importance to people of the bigger group, the tribe or the nation. In traditional societies, individuals tend to value the group over themselves, and to sacrifice their personal interests. In modern societies, these priorities are reversed.

The fourth item refers to criteria for position and status in society. In traditional societies it is extremely important which family one is born into, how old you are, whether you are male or female. In modern societies an individual's position is measured far more on merit − how skilled one is at one's job.

The fifth item in the table, functionally diffuse versus functionally specific, concerns the principle of structural differentiation. In modern societies, in other words, both individuals and institutions tend to be more specialized (and therefore more efficient).

The first thing that is immediately apparent about this set of dichotomies is that, as a description of modern society, one has to be very careful with them. Modern societies quite often incorporate personal, intimate, and face-to-face relationships even in the business of making money and being efficient. There are, for example, many family firms which operate extremely successfully in a highly competitive environment.

Another way to express this principle is to say that Parsons' description of traditional and modern societies is far too simplistic. It is not merely a case of one being the opposite of the other. Modern societies are mixtures of a range of different values, norms, and relationships. They are not purely or universally rational, universalistic or achievement-oriented, as modernization theory might have wanted.

The New Right: capitalism and neo-liberalism

If we consider the political motivations behind the origins of modernization theory, it is clear that a major part of it was designed to keep Third World countries away from the influence of Russian or Chinese communism. The third leg of modernization theory, then, namely its propagation of 'free market' solutions to development, was probably its most important leg. It was most blatantly here a political objective masquerading as an economic one.

The way in which this objective has expressed itself has shifted quite significantly in the post-World War II period. During the 1950s and 1960s the major proponents and the most active agents of capitalist development were particular First World countries, most notably the United States. Through the instrument of foreign aid, they promoted development and political allegiance.

During the 1980s and the 1990s this role has been taken over by the World Bank and the IMF. These two organizations have not only taken over the most energetic roles in promoting free market development, but they have also been the largest source of funding. Thus, between 1985 and 1996 the percentage of the United States' GNP devoted to foreign aid declined from 0,24 per cent to 0,12 per cent. (And the largest single recipient of this American contribution is Israel, which is not really a developing country at all (Todaro 2000: 593, 596).)

Free market, or (as they are currently called) neo-liberal, principles received very powerful political support during the 1980s with the accession to power of Margaret Thatcher in Great Britain and Ronald Reagan in the United States. At almost the same time, the World Bank, the IMF, and the World Trade Organization (WTO) were promoting very similar principles. Given this spread of agreement between governments and multilateral organizations, neo-liberalism was labelled 'the Washington consensus'.

What are these free market or capitalist or neo-liberal principles of development? In brief, they mean that states and state organizations should stay out of the market as far as possible. States should not intervene in the economy, they should not interfere with the unfettered working of demand and supply. State or parastatal organizations should not, as far as possible, be providing services (Todaro 2000: 95–9).

The reason behind this is quite simple. States and state employees are not bound by the 'discipline of the market'. That means that states and parastatal corporations do not go bankrupt if they perform inefficiently. They are guaranteed state funding. Because of this lack of sanction, state organizations, say neo-liberal economists, are typically either inefficient or corrupt or both (Preston 1997: 251ff).

It follows from this that states should remove themselves from the market, cut back on their spending, and privatize, that is sell off, as many of their operations as possible. Taxes should be lowered. Governments should decrease their borrowing, as this will decrease their spending (and lower their deficits). Where governments do intervene in the economy it should be to control inflation and the supply of money in the economy. Also they should limit the activities of trade unions, since these organizations tend to push up wages, which in their turn push up prices.

Neo-liberalism is the most influential leg of modernization theory. It has a dramatic impact on Third World countries today.

The same principle applies to the operation of private-sector corporations. To the extent that they are protected from the workings of the market, they will also be unprofitable, inefficient, and corrupt. Private corporations, just like states, should be subject to the discipline of the market. This implies that states should work to eliminate monopolistic conditions in the market, that is, where one or two large corporations dominate the market to such an extent that there is no longer real competition.

Governments should also encourage production for export. That means that they should eliminate, as far as possible, trade tariffs or customs duties which raise the price of goods coming into the country, or subsidies to goods made inside or leaving the country. And they should remove barriers to investment from foreign corporations entering the country.

The International Monetary Fund and the World Bank

The so-called 'Bretton Woods sisters', the International Monetary Fund (IMF) and the World Bank, have become very powerful purveyors of neo-liberal policies in the Third World. Originally the IMF was set up to deal with short-term financial crises in the world, while the World Bank was established to pursue longer term national development. During the debt crisis into which Third World countries fell during the 1980s, and the financial crises which befell a number of Third World countries in the 1990s, the IMF was almost the only available instrument of assistance. In addition to that, many commercial banks refused to help desperate Third World governments without IMF approval. However, the IMF would lend money only under certain circumstances, its so-called 'stabilization policies'. These were nothing more nor less than neo-liberal economics (Todaro 2000: 557, 572–5).

The World Bank, for its part, while pursuing national development projects, has also required governments to change their economic policies as a condition for assistance. These are known as 'structural adjustment programmes' (SAPs), but they have also been in line with neo-liberal policies.

While debate has raged around these stabilization policies and SAPs, for our purposes what is important is that both of these policies have caused serious distress for poorer people in Third World countries. Government welfare services, such as health and education, have been cut, and prices of food have risen very sharply. In a number of countries there have serious political upheavals following IMF and World Bank action (Todaro 2000: 98).

Criticisms of neo-liberalism

Neo-liberalism has not gone unchallenged. As its very evident failures became clear there was mounting criticism from a number of quarters, but probably most coherently from Keynesians. Named after the English economist, John Maynard Keynes, this stream of thinking starts with a very different assessment of the role of the free market. For Keynesians, the free market is a profoundly flawed mechanism. It does not produce the growth or the employment that neo-liberals claim for it. In fact, it tends to worsen levels of inequality and unemployment (Preston 1996: 251ff).

In addition, capitalism is extremely unstable, lurching from boom to depression with depressing regularity. In these circumstances it is the job of states to intervene in the economy quite actively and, more particularly, to spend money in order to stimulate demand and growth in the economy. It is up to states to protect the position of poorer citizens by establishing welfare benefits such as unemployment insurance, education, minimum wages, and water and electricity. Keynesians also expect the government to nationalize certain services in order to guarantee service provision (Todaro 2000).

You will have noticed that Keynesians end up with proposals which are the exact opposite of those of the neo-liberals in many ways. Their criticisms have

been amply assisted by the very evident failures of the IMF and World Bank's neo-liberal policies.

Perhaps the main reason why neo-liberal policies have been so bad is that they work with inflexible models which are applied without consideration of local circumstances. And that, in turn, is caused by the fact that conventional free market assumptions do not fully apply in Third World countries:

> *The problem is that many LDC (less developed country) economies are so different in structure and organization from their Western counterparts that the behavioral assumptions and policy precepts of traditional neoclassical theory are sometimes questionable and often incorrect* (Todaro 2000: 98).

Neo-liberal development in South Africa

Since the political transformation of South Africa through democratic elections in 1994, there has been considerable debate around economic policy for the country. The local debate has mirrored the international debate. There have been neo-liberals, on the one hand, who have argued for following free market principles. These principles have been spelled out in the Growth, Employment, and Redistribution Programme (GEAR) published in 1996. On the other hand, the Keynesians and Socialists have argued for greater regulation of the inequal-ities and inequities of the free market. These principles were originally spelled out in the Reconstruction and Development Programme (RDP) published in 1994. On the whole, the South African Government, despite the radical and socialist origins of many of its members, has followed neo-liberal principles quite closely. (Nelson Mandela, on his release from prison in 1990, shocked the free marketers when he said, 'the nationalization of the mines, banks, and monopoly industry is the policy of the ANC.' The policy of the ANC has shifted considerably since then (Marais 2001: 124).)

Let us consider some of these issues in more detail.

The South African Government, following neo-liberal principles, has made plans, for example, to sell off state assets such as South African Airways (SAA) and Telkom in order to get the state out of the private sector, and to contribute to the budget from such sales. They have brought down the budget deficit in order to decrease state spending and further limit the extent of its intervention in the economy. They have attempted to keep inflation down to between 3 per cent and 6 per cent in order to stabilize the economy and keep down prices of basic goods for poorer people. They have eliminated import tariffs and other forms of protection in line with the recommendations of the World Trade Organization, since these controls make for inefficient competition. And they have plans in place to phase out over time state controls over the international flow of finance (Coetzee et al 2001: 218–20).

Despite its socialist roots, the ANC Government in South Africa has followed neo-liberal economic policies.

South African Keynesians and socialists, on the other hand, have called for increased state spending, both for welfare (in health, housing, and education) purposes, and to boost economic activity. As a result they have called for a bigger budget deficit. They have wanted increased protection for labour and provision for the unemployed. They have opposed privatization since this could increase unemployment. They have been extremely suspicious of the World Bank and the IMF's involvement in South Africa. And they have urged a more rapid redistribution of land to black farmers and the landless.

The debate on macro-economic policy in South Africa continues to swing back and forth. For further detail on this see the works by Marais and Coetzee (Marais 2001; Coetzee et al 2001).

Conclusion

In this chapter we have examined the three legs of modernization theory: *evolutionism*, *functionalism*, and *capitalism* or *neo-liberalism*. As an evolutionist writer, Parsons is much more sophisticated than Rostow. If evolutionism is defined by five characteristics of social change: namely, that it happens gradually, in a set number of stages and hence repeatably, irreversibly, progressively, and tends towards the same point – if these are the basic principles of evolutionism, then all five of them have been demolished by subsequent writers. There is some hope for the notion that social change can be directional, but this new line jettisons all of the biological foundations of old evolutionist thinking.

Functionalism emphasizes the centrality of value consensus in holding society together. Parsons presents a series of values and social relationships which define traditional as against modern societies. These are problematic, since modern society is presented as being too pure and unmixed. It still contains much that is traditional.

Capitalism as the final, and maybe, key characteristic of modernization theory has been taken up by the IMF and World Bank in the 1980s and 1990s.

3 Theories of Underdevelopment

In Marxist and neo-Marxist theories, Third World countries are at the mercy of First World initiatives. They exist in a global system shaped by First World needs.

Introduction

In this chapter we consider the various theories which have arisen from neo-Marxist thinking. I call it 'neo-Marxist' rather than 'Marxist', because in many ways it contradicts both what Marx himself wrote and what 'orthodox' Marxists would think. Marx himself thought that developing countries would follow the paths which developed countries had followed. (In this respect he was very similar to modernization theorists.) Later neo-Marxist thinkers, however, have thought that developing countries would follow a very different path. The reason is that these 'newer' countries had been placed into a global system. In that system they would remain permanently and actively underdeveloped. As we shall see, Marx failed to take account of the world system as a unit. Seeing developed and developing countries, rich and poor, as both part of a system in relationship to one another, makes a considerable difference to the freedom of movement enjoyed by poorer countries.

Neo-Marxist thinking on development has, over a long period of time, been a most fertile area. It has spawned a wide range of theories to explain under-development. A slightly pruned-down list includes:
- theories of imperialism;
- dependency theory;
- world system theory;
- new international division of labour (NIDL) theory, and
- regulation theory.

Each of these theories tries to go beyond and improve on the previous one. Sometimes, as we shall see, one theory's critique of another is quite valid. At other times, historical circumstances have changed, so that each theory can be allocated to a quite specific time and place. Dependency theory, for example, is most relevant and valid for the colonial and immediate post-colonial period – from approximately 1880 to 1960. NIDL theory, in contrast, applies to a later period (1970s and 1980s). In these cases, then, later theories are not necessarily better than earlier ones. They simply apply to a different set of circumstances.

Neo-Marxist theories have all grappled with two central issues. The first is the role of politics and culture in society. Neo-Marxism has inherited from Marxism its heavy emphasis on economics. For both neo-Marxists and Marxists economics is the determinant part of society. Politics and culture are, mistak-enly, seen as weak reflections of a basic economic reality. (See my discussion of this issue in the first book of this series, *What is Sociology?,* page 34.) *We* shall see how later theories, such as regulation theory, attempt to rectify this problem of *economic determinism.*

The second issue that neo-Marxist theories have struggled with is the rapid development of East Asian countries after World War II. Being sceptical of, and pessimistic about, the possibilities of proper development under capitalism, neo-Marxist theories have at times been caught unawares by the strength of East Asian development. We shall see how they have adapted periodically to take account of this reality.

Whereas neo-Marxists have battled with economic determinism and with East Asian development, they have been good at one thing: unlike modernization theorists, they have realized the importance of globalization. We shall see that both dependency theory and world system theory stressed the key principle that both developed and underdeveloped countries form part of the same global system.

So, with these three themes – economic determinism, East Asian development, and globalization – in mind, let us consider neo-Marxist theories of under-development.

The capitalist need for empire: theories of imperialism

Imperialism is about the growth of empires. It indicates the control and/or conquest of one or more countries by another. A common understanding of imperialism arises from our knowledge of the Roman Empire. In this notion one country gradually expands its sphere of control by conquest of its surrounding territories. In Rome's case it gradually spread its way around the Mediterranean Sea, eventually to incorporate large parts of Europe, the Middle East, and Great Britain. The process of conquest can continue for a great length of time and over vast expanses of territory.

Empires expand for particular reasons. There is a certain dynamic which drives them ever outward. For Rome, this was the need for slaves in their production systems. War and conquest produced a great many prisoners of war who were then inducted into slavery. In addition, there was the need for more land for agricultural production, and competition for political power between various classes or between individuals within the empire. Certainly Roman generals spent a huge amount of time fighting one another!

Marxist theories of *imperialism* concentrate their attentions on imperialism under the capitalist system, that is starting in the nineteenth century and continuing into the twentieth century. Capitalist imperialism is imperialism of a particular kind. It is driven by a very particular capitalist dynamic. That is the need, indeed the urgency, for capital to break out of one specific country and to spread itself to others which are under that country's control. Quite simply, capitalism in Europe was producing too many goods to be consumed by its national popu-lation. In other words, there were the twin problems of underconsumption and overproduction. Capitalism needed to expand its sphere of operations to incor-porate other markets, new sources of cheap labour and raw materials, and new

Lenin's theory of imperialism differs in quite fundamental ways from later neo-Marxists' theories of development.

opportunities for investment. (There was considerable debate among Marxist writers of the time as to which factor was most important – the search for new markets, for cheap labour, or for new investment opportunities.)

The most famous writer on imperialism is Lenin, the first leader of Soviet Russia. In his pamphlet, *Imperialism: The Highest Stage of Capitalism* (1916), Lenin argued that competition among companies in the market had led to their amalgamation into ever larger and larger corporations that were dominating the market to such an extent that there was effectively no more competition. This was *monopoly capitalism*.

In the rise to power of monopoly capital, banks had played a critical part in providing finance. Banks were indeed then so powerful that a fusion had taken place between bankers and industrialists to form what Lenin termed 'finance capital'. And it was finance capital which, in its drive to solve the problems of underconsumption and overproduction, pressured governments into imperialist expansion. The conquest of colonial territories, in Africa, Latin American, and Asia, then, provided opportunities for the exportation of this underutilized capital.

However, there was severe competition among countries for new territories. Competition between companies had been complicated by international competition. And this new competition was so intense that it engendered war. (Note that Lenin's pamphlet was written during World War I.) For Lenin it was, of course, the working class of each nation which would be drafted to fight their wars. The aim of his pamphlet was to persuade such working classes not to fight and hence to weaken capitalism and thus create the conditions which would lead to socialist revolution. Figure 3.1 below sketches the steps in Lenin's argument which led from the concentration of capital and the growing influence of banks through several steps eventually to a prediction of war.

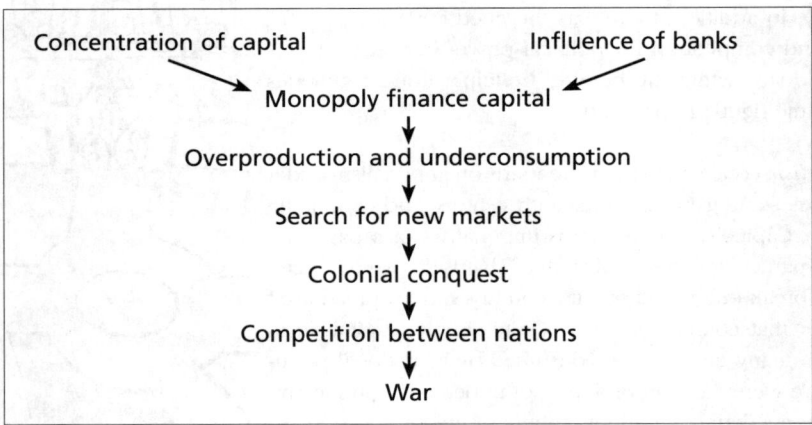

Fig 3.1: Lenin's theory of imperialism

Whatever Lenin's specific ingenious plans to subvert the capitalist system, we need to note three main things about his analysis. First, he was examining the movements and dynamics of capital within Europe. He paid very little attention to the effect of this capital in the colonized territories. We shall see that subsequent Marxist writers spent much more time examining the (destructive) impact which capital had on the economic, political and cultural life of such colonies. In other words, using more recent terminology, theories of imperialism focus on First World countries. Theories of underdevelopment, which we will discuss further on, focus on Third World countries.

Secondly, such attention as Lenin did pay to colonial areas predicted that the influence of capital there would be to move those countries into fully fledged capitalism. Here Lenin was following Marx himself when he said:

> *The country that is more developed industrially only shows, to the less developed, the image of its own future* (Marx 1976: 91).

We shall see that later Marxist writers turned that principle around. They argued that capitalism effectively and actively *under*-developed the colonies. It purposely blocked the movement of those countries to mature capitalism and condemned them to a form of distorted development.

Thirdly, Lenin's argument was that European colonial powers exported capital to the colonies. That is, it was a matter of investment. Later Marxist writers, in contrast, saw underdeveloped countries as suffering from a *lack* of sufficient capital investment. To them trade was a more important factor in explaining underdevelopment.

The ravages of colonialism: dependency theory

There is a gap of some 50 years between the writings of Lenin on imperialism in 1916 and the appearance of the dependency perspective in the 1960s. That gap indicates also a considerable gap in the understanding of how development and underdevelopment happened in the Third World. We have already indicated some of the differences between the orthodox Marxism of Lenin and later neo-Marxist dependency writers. We shall see that there are many more such differences between dependency writers and 'orthodox' Marxists.

But dependency theorists did not only differ from orthodox Marxists. They also differed quite vehemently from modernization theorists. It is important to note that dependency theory originated in the context of the Cold War and that a great many of the writers involved in its conceptualization were from the Third World. We saw earlier that modernization theory was used as an ideological weapon in the West's fight against communism. Dependency theory was itself a political response to this tactic, from Third World writers, criticizing the impact of Western First World countries on their development.

Dependency theory received its most significant intellectual boost from work done by Latin American writers. The best known among them are Raul Prebisch, Theotonio dos Santos, Fernando Cardoso, and Enso Faletto. From the African continent there were writers such as Walter Rodney and Samir Amin. From America there were Paul Baran and Peter Sweezy. However, the person who did most to popularize dependency theory was the American economist, André Gunder Frank. Through a series of books, starting with *Capitalism and Underdevelopment in Latin America* in 1967, his name became almost synonymous with dependency theory.

In a nutshell, dependency theorists argued that the world is divided between wealthier core countries and poorer peripheral countries, and that core countries are responsible for an active and purposive underdevelopment of peripheral countries. In dependency theory, underdevelopment is not a case of countries that 'got left behind' in the march of progress, as modernization theory liked to suggest. They were explicitly held back.

Let us examine this in more detail. For dependency theory, the nature of being 'held back' was structural. That means that the economies and societies of peripheral countries showed a distorted form of capitalism. The structures of these societies had been shaped in order to service the needs of core countries more efficiently. Much as a potter shapes the soft clay of a pot in order to perform a specific function, so peripheral societies had been moulded as an extension of core economies.

It is important for understanding the notion of dependency that we distinguish it clearly from the notion of *dependence* or *interdependence*. One country may be dependent on another for the delivery of some service or product. There is no country in the world that is not dependent on another for something. But that does not mean that there is a *dependency* relationship. The fact that Japan is dependent on another country for the delivery of oil does not mean that Japan suffers distorted development. Lesotho, in southern Africa, however, is quite a different case. The Lesotho economy is substantially geared to the provision of migrant labour to South African mines. The whole country has been shaped for that purpose. This is a dependency relationship.

What does this relationship look like? The answer depends on the historical period we are talking about because dependency theory writers often see the core–periphery relationship going through a number of stages, such as: *merchant capitalism, colonialism proper,* and *neo-colonialism.* What remains constant, however, is the subordination of the periphery to core needs, the function one performs for the other. Let us take the first stage – merchant capitalism – as an example.

Dependency refers to a position of structural distortion in the economy of a Third World.

Merchant capitalism, as the name implies, was dominated by trade, but trade of a particularly violent kind, often accompanied by armed pillage. I am speaking here of slavery, the trade in human beings. Over a period of 200 years almost 9 million African people were transported across the Atlantic Ocean to work on commercial plantations in the West Indies and the American colonies. Of those about 2 million died on the way over (Webster 1990: 70–81).

While there is some dispute over the numbers involved in this human tragedy, what is significant for our purposes are the structures which resulted from this activity. Trade in slaves was not a new thing in Africa before the arrival of the Europeans. But the previously existing slave trade had been more limited in numbers, and had connected the west coast of Africa with northern neighbours across the Sahara Desert. Now trade was oriented outwards towards the coast. This mercantile stage of colonialism lasted until the middle of the nineteenth century.

The second dependency phase was that of *colonialism proper*. It is important to understand that, during this phase, peripheral economies operated to supply raw materials (plus the cheap labour to produce it) to core economies. In other words, peripheral economies were primarily export oriented. They exported agricultural and mining goods (that is raw materials) in exchange for manufactured goods. Newly elected political leaders could and did benefit from their associations with large multinational corporations. Dependency theorists called them the *comprador* (or translator) bourgeoisie. They assisted multinationals and Western governments in the exploitation of their own countries. In colonial countries during this period, urban development, transport systems, forms of government, and labour patterns were all geared to serve that one primary function, and it was a function that benefited the core.

We have seen now how through the various phases of colonialism the basic economic structures of colonial societies were laid down and maintained. But we need to ask ourselves why this was necessarily disadvantageous to peripheral countries. After all, these countries were benefiting from the colonial construction of road and railway networks. New education systems had been set up. Many of the colonial elite had been educated in Europe, at the best universities in the world. Legal, administrative, and financial systems had been established. So what was the problem?

Mechanisms of underdevelopment

For dependency theorists there were three main mechanisms which contributed to underdevelopment. The first and most important of these was the unequal balance of trade. As we have seen, peripheral economies exported primary goods and imported manufactured goods. However, the prices of primary goods (agriculture and mining) tend to fall over time, whereas the prices of manufactured goods tend to rise. Over a number of years, therefore, there was an unequal balance between exported primary goods and imported manufactured goods. In short, money was being sucked out of peripheral economies through unfavourable trading relationships.

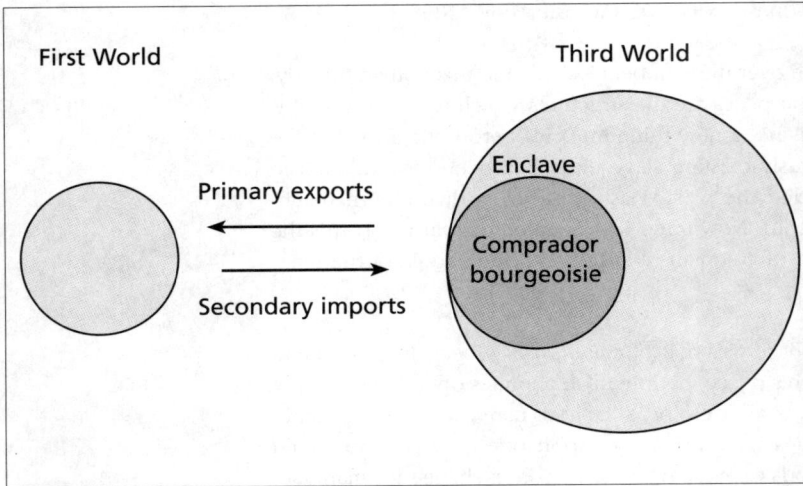

Fig 3.2: The dependency relationship

The second aspect of underdevelopment was the lack of investment from multinational corporations in expanding their operations in colonial countries. What development there was took place in isolated enclaves. There were minimal ripple effects into the local economy. Foreign corporations in Third World countries were there to benefit from extremely cheap labour (and we will see why it was so cheap in a moment). But they did nothing to train this labour. They did nothing to add value to the goods being produced. In other words, raw, unprocessed goods were being exported.

The third mechanism of 'surplus extraction' was the use of extremely cheap migrant labour. This labour was cheap because it comprised single men who oscillated between rural and urban areas. They left their families behind in the rural areas. Once their employment contracts were completed, they returned to their families and their farming operations. Now, employers argued that these were men whose families were being supported by their extended kinship groups and by their families' farming activities. As a result, employers did not need to pay wages to support rural families, but only the single man. That made for very low wages and some quite brutal inducements on people to work.

Given these mechanisms of surplus extraction, dependency theorists argued that peripheral countries were being blocked in their development by the activities of core countries. Worse than that, however, there was very little prospect of their ever becoming developed. For what had been established in peripheral countries was a sterile and empty form of capitalism. And it was sterile because it had been drafted into the service of core countries. You will remember that Marx and Lenin believed that, after an initial period of disruption, capitalism would grow and prosper in Third World countries. Dependency theorists rejected this analysis. The only way out for peripheral countries, they said, was the overthrow of the capitalist system.

There was, however, one serious problem with dependency theory: it was so pessimistic. For dependency theory there was no hope of development outside of the overthrow of the capitalist system. But, particularly from the 1970s onwards, it was clear that certain peripheral countries were growing at quite dramatic rates. This was especially true of the four East Asian 'tigers', South Korea, Taiwan, Singapore, and Hong Kong. This was something that dependency theory simply could not explain.

Dependent development: world system theory

Immanuel Wallerstein, an American economic historian, is the father of world system theory. His work appeared at much the same time as that of André Gunder Frank's. His most important work, *The Modern World System*, appeared in three volumes from 1974 to 1989. In many ways these two writers shared a basic understanding of how underdevelopment worked and we shall investigate these aspects in a moment. What is more important for our purposes are the differences between their viewpoints. For world system theory was much less pessimistic about the possibilities of development in the Third World than dependency theory. World system theory made provision for significant development to occur in peripheral countries despite relationships of dependency. How was this supposed to happen?

Both the dependency and the world system theories saw underdevelopment as based on unequal trade between countries.

First, where Frank saw a two-way division of the world into core and periphery, Wallerstein saw a three-way division of the world into *core, semi-periphery*, and *periphery*. Wallerstein thought that certain countries operated as intermediaries between core and peripheral countries. Such semi-peripheral countries were exploited by core countries, but also had their own spheres of influence which they in turn exploited. In other words, semi-peripheral countries had their own peripheries. In the context of the Americas, for example, the United States was the core country. Brazil operated as a semi-peripheral intermediary through which United States influence was filtered into Latin America. And there were a range of Latin American countries which fell within Brazil's sphere of influence. Brazil was the intermediary that both exploited and was exploited. That was why it is called *dependent development*.

What is important about this new division of the world, for Wallerstein, was that he foresaw the possibility that certain peripheral countries might change their position to the semi-periphery. Brazil was just such a country which had shifted its rank position in the world.

Such a move, said Wallerstein, was not easy. Countries could not move just when they liked. It depended a great deal on the fluctuations in the world economy and on the efforts of national governments. World War II had been just such a fluctuation which had provided the opportunity for certain countries to move.

South Africa is one country that was able to make use of this opening and move up from periphery to semi-periphery during the period 1933 to 1955. During that time South Africa significantly expanded its manufacturing industry away from its reliance on agriculture and mining. The value of manufacturing production leapt from R780 million in 1946–1947 to R2,2 billion in 1954–1955. South Africa's Gross Domestic Product climbed from R550,8 million in 1933 to R989 million in 1940 (Horwitz 1967: 232–9).

At the same time, South Africa's tentacles spread into the sub-continent. The number of migrant workers from southern African countries is an index of this influence. By 1961 almost a quarter of a million workers were coming into the country, mainly from two sources, Mozambique and Lesotho (Lipton 1985). More interestingly, by the 1960s South Africa had also produced at least one multinational corporation of global scale. In the early 1980s Anglo American Corporation, through its subsidiary Minorco, was the largest single foreign investor in the United States, ahead of oil companies Shell and BP (Innes 1984). Innes comments on South Africa's shift during this period as follows:

> Over the past hundred years (South Africa) has transformed itself from an underdeveloped chattel of imperialism into an aggressive imperialist power which exhibits many of the characteristics of a monopoly capitalist society (Innes 1984: 241).

The most famous example of movement through the various world system levels, however, is Japan, which since the 1860s has moved from the world economic periphery right up to the core. By the 1980s Japan was the world's second largest economy. In world system terms, the four East Asian tigers, Taiwan, South Korea, Hong Kong, and Singapore, operated as Japan's semi-periphery, whereas other East Asian economies, in turn, functioned as their regional periphery.

Problems with dependency theory and world system theory

I mentioned above that orthodox Marxists did not like dependency theorists. They did not like world system theorists any better. The reason was that for both Frank and Wallerstein capitalist exploitation worked by way of an unequal *trade* relationship, that is, cheap raw materials in exchange for expensive manufactured goods.

Now, for conventional Marxists, exploitation happens by way of *class* exploitation. The ruling class exploits the working class by paying them less than their labour time is worth. This is, for them, the essence of capitalism. Trading relationships between countries are simply a secondary result of this primary class relationship. Or, put differently, capitalist exploitation is about class, not about trade.

How, then, did this class exploitation occur in Third World countries, according to orthodox Marxists? You will remember that, in discussing dependency theory previously, we described how capitalists in Third World countries used the existence of rural families and rural resources to justify very low wages paid to migrant workers. For orthodox Marxists this was a case of the exploitation of workers, but with a difference. In this case there was an 'articulation' between two different modes of production, a capitalist and a pre-capitalist mode. The capitalist mode was able to use the continued existence of a pre-capitalist or subsistence economy in order to lower its wages significantly. For orthodox Marxists, that was an important *class* basis on which core countries were able to build their exploitation of peripheral countries (Wolpe 1972; Foster-Carter 1978).

Apart from the criticism that orthodox Marxists had of world system theory (and of dependency theory), there is another important point of criticism. World system theory was still quite a pessimistic theory. Inasmuch as core countries exploited peripheral countries by means of unequal trade, world system theory relied on the fact that peripheral countries continued to produce only raw materials.

Now, in the 1970s it became increasingly evident that the economies of Third World countries in general, and East Asian countries in particular, were no longer limited to the primary production of raw materials. These economies had developed substantial manufacturing sectors. This was something that world system theory found difficult to explain. Once more, Marxist development theory needed to shift in order to accommodate a new phenomenon. Hence the arrival of new international division of labour (NIDL) theory.

False hopes: new international division of labour theory

NIDL theory became known in the late 1970s through the work of Volker Fröbel and his associates in Germany, through their book entitled *The New International Division of Labour*. They chose this (somewhat clumsy) name because they thought that an old division of labour in the world had been replaced by a new one. In the old dispensation the world had been divided between core countries, which produced manufactured goods, and peripheral countries, which produced primary goods. That old division of labour was now being replaced by a new one in which peripheral countries were also producing manufactured goods. This was the way in which Marxist theory was going to explain the spectacular rise of East Asian economies.

How did this development come about? In brief, argued Fröbel, economic conditions in Europe had turned against multinational corporations (MNCs) in the 1970s. Labour was becoming much more expensive. MNCs were therefore moving their manufacturing operations to the Third World in search of cheaper labour while maintaining their original headquarters in Europe. Let us look at this more carefully.

During the 1960s, labour had been moving from southern European countries, such as Turkey and Greece, to work in the more prosperous economies of the north. Those previously migrant workers had, however, settled in Europe, joined trade unions, and themselves become expensive. Where workers had earlier moved to find factories, now factories began to move to Third World countries to employ cheap labour.

This kind of move had not been possible in the past. But new forms of communication and transportation had become available. In addition, the new products being produced in the Third World were easy to transport, namely textiles and computers. In this way a computer company might have its headquarters in Silicon Valley, California, where important planning, research and development, and marketing took place. But the manufacture and assembly of the actual product could take place in a country on the other side of the globe. Investment in industrial plants in Third World countries grew at an extremely rapid rate from the 1970s onwards: from US$2,4 billion in 1962, to US$11 billion in 1980, to US$35 billion in 1990, and then up to US$120 billion in 1997 (Todaro 2000: 578).

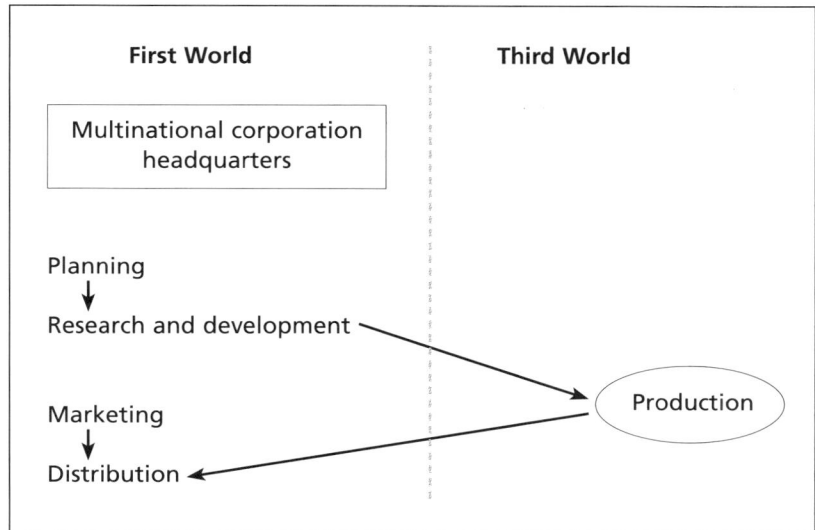

Fig 3.3: NIDL view of dependent development

Despite its novelty, NIDL theorists were still sceptical about this form of development. First of all, a large proportion of the people working in these factories were women. Often they were recent migrants from rural to urban areas, and therefore quite traditional in their views. In consequence, these women found it difficult to question patriarchal authority or to organize trade unions. As a result, their wages were significantly lower than those for men. Here was a case, said NIDL theory, of the 'super-exploitation' of labour.

In addition, many of these new factories were located in export processing zones (EPZs). These were areas specifically designated by a government for the establishment of manufacturing plants. Companies which invested in these areas enjoyed a range of special advantages. Thus, for example, they might not pay import tariffs, they might pay much lower taxation, there might be restrictions on the activities of trade unions, or there might be rebates on a range of other investments. In other words, said NIDL theorists (much as dependency theorists had said before them), very little development was rippling outwards into the local economy. It was an all too recognizable case of *enclave development*.

Problems with NIDL

Whereas NIDL theory had been a considerable improvement on the dependency and world system theories in explaining what had been happening in the Far East, it soon became clear that NIDL was itself far too pessimistic. It was unable to apply itself to a number of extremely important developments.

One of the most obvious of these developments was the rise of very powerful multinational corporations in Third World countries. A significant number of the tigers in East Asia did not need foreign MNCs to establish manufacturing plants in their countries. They were doing it themselves. For example, following the way Japan had done it, in the 1960s the South Korean Government launched a number of parastatal companies, called *chaebols*. These quite rapidly grew into very substantial MNCs such as Samsung, Daewoo, Kia, and Hyundai, and were set free from government control. They were central in driving the development of South Korea forward.

A second problem with NIDL theory has been its *economic determinism*. That means that, much like other neo-Marxist theories, NIDL theorists have focused strongly on economic matters to the neglect of cultural and political factors. It is significant that one of the fastest-growing economies in the world is not a country but a cultural constellation. I am referring here to the dramatic growth of the east coast of China (the provinces of Guangdong and Fujian), in combination with Taiwan, Hong Kong, and the Chinese diaspora. (A diaspora is the population of a country who live permanently outside the borders of that country.) They have mobilized what Castells calls *guanxi* capitalism. This refers to the cross-border family ties among Chinese communities in the region which have been used to further investment and economic activity (Mittelman 1995; Castells 2000).

NIDL theory spotted the fact that manufacturing plants were being transferred to peripheral countries.

At the same time, national governments have been central to the development process. Ever since the Meiji restoration in Japan in the 1860s the Japanese Government has been driving the modernization process, planning, guiding, stimulating research, providing investment and protection. Many of the successful East Asian economies have explicitly followed this model.

In addition, there has been significant cooperation between states in the region. The ASEÂN (Association of South East Asian Nations) group comprising Thailand, Indonesia, Malaysia, and the Philippines is a well-known one. The Japanese policy of regional development, often referred to as 'the flying geese policy', is another example (Mittelman 1995).

In short, both cultural and political factors have been absolutely crucial to the development of the Far East. It is not enough to focus only on the dynamics of capitalism.

Unstable capitalism: regulation theory

This is a good point for us to consider a more recent Marxist theory, namely, regulation theory. This theory has grown from the writings of Michel Aglietta in *A Theory of Capitalist Regulation: The US Experience* (1979) and Alain Lipietz in *Mirages and Miracles* (1987).

Regulation theory starts from the principle that capitalism is an inherently unstable and unpredictable system. Throughout the twentieth century, for example, there have been recurrent booms followed by depressions in the world economy. The most recent of these started at the end of 2001. At that time, Japan, the world's second largest economy, had been in recession for more than a decade. A number of East Asian economies had been devastated by the 1997–1998 currency crises. In the United States the stock exchange had plummeted following the bursting of the so-called 'dot.com' bubble in 2001. This was followed by the attack on the World Trade Centre on 11 September 2001.

In such circumstances, say regulation theorists, many people are concerned to implement controls on this instability, in other words, to apply some measure of regulation. In consequence there are currently both international bodies and national governments that actively intervene in economies in an attempt to avoid recession and promote booms. The International Monetary Fund is one such body, the prime function of which is to stabilize the world economy. But this is not easy. For capitalism shifts continually in the way in which production occurs and capital is accumulated. Regulation theorists therefore talk of changing *regimes of accumulation*.

There are indeed periods of time when national governments, with or without international bodies, manage successfully to regulate a particular regime of accumulation. This they call a *mode of regulation*. A national or world economic boom occurs, then, when regulatory bodies successfully combine a particular mode of regulation with a particular regime of accumulation, that is, a successful regulation occurs. Given the instability of the system, this combination cannot last very long. Then a new regime of accumulation takes over and a new mode of regulation must be found.

Let us take an example. In Aglietta's analysis of the American economy, the economic depression of the 1930s and 1940s was followed by a boom in the 1950s and 1960s. This was brought about by a Fordist regime of accumulation. Fordism was characterized by assembly-line mass production of goods, rising wages, and detailed supervision of labour. Workers found themselves doing minutely specialized and tediously repetitive jobs on a moving conveyor belt. This form of production was named after Henry Ford, whose Ford Motor Company had launched the Model T Ford in 1908, the first motor car affordable to a wide American consumer public. By his improvements in the efficiency of the production system Ford was able to bring down the price of the Model T from US$850 in 1908 to US$260 in 1925 (Aglietta 1979).

This form of production, however, was substantially supported by the United States Government of the time under Roosevelt. During the 1930s and 1940s, and contrary to free market principles, the United States Government spent large amounts of money on launching public works programmes, in establishing unemployment insurance, and in other kinds of poverty relief.

Regulation theory is a considerable improvement on earlier neo-Marxist theories.

Government spending, then, supplemented the rising income of American workers. United States economic policy took its inspiration at the time from the work of British economist, John Maynard Keynes.

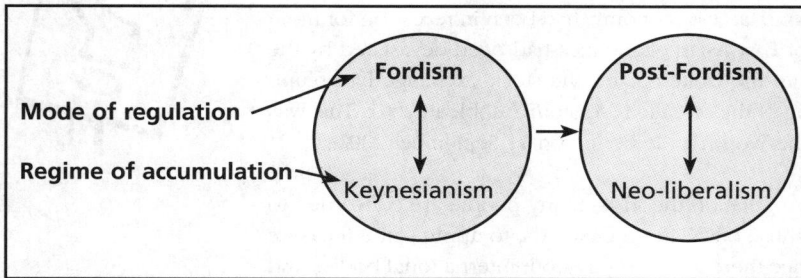

Fig 3.4: From Fordism to post-Fordism

Here, then, was the combination of a Fordist regime of accumulation with a Keynesian mode of regulation and rising consumer demand which worked spectacularly well for the United States economy. The combination, adjusted for different circumstances, spread also to other countries. Many countries in Europe followed suit. The result was a worldwide boom during the 1960s.

What happened to the Third World through all of this? Regulation theorists are unsympathetic to previous neo-Marxist versions of parasitic core–periphery relationships. After all, connections with Third World countries mean very little to First World countries. The overwhelming proportion of their international trade is with other First World countries. Third World countries, say regulation theorists, have simply failed to make the transition to full-scale capitalism. They are stuck in distorted forms anchored by inappropriate government policies and corrupt politicians.

South Africa's racial Fordism likewise got stuck because of a very limited market demand. During the 1950s and 1960s South Africa's economy participated in the worldwide boom. But over many years the country's apartheid policy had had the effect of concentrating the benefits of growth in the white section of the population. Being only a small part of the total population, their buying power was also limited. Once this limit had been reached, the country's production was substantially hamstrung (Gelb 1991).

During the 1970s, however, the hitherto successful combination of Fordism and Keynesianism collapsed. The crisis was triggered by a dramatic rise in the prices of oil and gold in the mid-1970s, and by changing consumer tastes. Consumers no longer wanted identical mass-produced goods. They were demanding differentiated and individualized products. They were asking for what we today call 'designer' products. In addition, the profitability of the 'golden' years had multiplied the number of participants in a growing market. Competition in the market had sharpened significantly and companies could no longer afford to keep raising wages.

Robust tigers: the rise of post-Fordism

During the 1980s, then, a new combination of accumulation and regulation arose, a combination between post-Fordist production, neo-liberal government policies, and a consumer public demanding individualized products. Let us consider what each of these elements meant.

Much like Fordism, the post-Fordist method of production arose in an automobile company, but this time it was a Japanese company, Toyota, rather than an American one. The central characteristic of the post-Fordist production system is its flexibility, that is, its ability to shift through a variety of products very rapidly. Where Henry Ford's assembly lines had been able to produce huge numbers of identical cars, Toyota's factories could switch from the production of one model to that of another quite quickly. The reason for this was twofold. Its workers were multiskilled and could perform a variety of skilled tasks. And its machines, being computer-driven, could be reprogrammed for a variety of jobs. In consequence, post-Fordist companies could be extremely sensitive to changing, and quite particular, consumer tastes (Haralambos & Holborn 1995: 214–18).

Supporting this worker and machine flexibility was the principle of 'just-in-time' (JIT) delivery by component manufacturers. Component manufacturers in the automobile industry supply the various parts of the motor car to the factory: batteries, windscreen wipers, tyres, or radios. In the post-Fordist system these manufacturers have to be equally flexible to match market shifts. They need to be able to change their production lines very rapidly and deliver with very short deadlines.

Under post-Fordism, relationships between management and labour were also sharply different from those under Fordism. Under Fordism, workers had been subjected to detailed and strict supervision by a multilayered hierarchy of management. They had worked as individuals confronted by the moving assembly line. In contrast, under post-Fordism, they worked much more as independent teams, each team responsible for a spread of tasks, often constructing a whole car, instead of tightening one screw on one wheel. In addition, management hierarchies were flatter and more consultative. In many cases, workers were encouraged to make suggestions to management on how to improve working conditions and efficient performance.

While this might sound like a huge improvement for labour, there was a substantial downside to it all. In conditions of ferocious competition for small niche markets many companies resorted to *downsizing* and *outsourcing*. What that meant was that the number of permanent workers was substantially reduced, and companies increased the number of casual and temporary workers. In addition, a range of jobs were subcontracted out to smaller companies. The result of this was, for significant numbers of workers, a decrease in wages, a loss of security and benefits, and the weakening of trade unions (Haralambos & Holborn 1995: 214–18).

Post-Fordism and the Third World

What are the implications of these innovations for development in the Third World? Here we need to be careful because the results were extremely varied. Some countries benefited hugely, particularly those in the Far East. Others, such as those in Africa, did not. Some industries, such as the automotive industry, had a very positive impact on their Third World hosts, others such as textiles and computers, did less well.

The reasons for this are both technical and political. The technical reasons have to do with the post-Fordist production system itself. Remember that flexible production relies also on flexible component manufacturers who can deliver their products at very short notice. What this means in many cases is that component manufacturers in the automotive industry have to be located close to the main assembly plant. Setting up an motor-car factory in another country means, then, also setting up 200 or more component providers in the same country. Now, that has huge implications for levels of employment, investment and technological expertise in that country (Gereffi 1994; Hill 1994).

The political reasons for the varied impact of development have to do with Japanese plans for regional development in the Far East. During the 1980s Japanese automobile production was challenging American production on a global scale. In 1980, for example, Japanese output had reached 11 million units compared to 8 million from the United States (Cohen 2000: 69). By way of response, the United States Government in 1985 resorted to protectionist measures. It imposed strict quotas on certain goods being imported into the United States. The way round this for Japanese motor-car manufacturers was to establish factories not only in the United States itself but also in other Third World countries. In this latter case the motor cars were no longer Japanese goods, but Korean or Singaporean. These countries then became 'export platforms' from which Japanese companies could circumvent United States import quotas (Hill 1994).

In addition to this, the Japanese Government had for many years had a policy of transferring its ageing mature technologies to other countries in the region. This was the so-called 'flying geese' policy. Geese typically fly in a V-formation, with one lead goose cutting the wind while others fly in its slipstream.

Transferred to the world of production, this pattern implied that Japan would be the lead goose, in terms of technological innovation, research, and design. As this technology declined in profitability, it was then passed down the chain to a second tier of countries whose labour costs were lower. These countries in turn could pass this down to a third and a fourth level.

The impact of all of these technical and political factors was that countries in the Japanese sphere of influence benefited substantially from their regional association. They did not, of course, all benefit equally. The so-called 'tigers', namely South Korea, Taiwan, Singapore, and Hong Kong, benefited first and most strongly. The 'second team', the so-called 'dragons', Thailand, Indonesia, Malaysia, and the Philippines, also benefited, but not quite to the same extent. Further down the line are countries such as China and Vietnam.

Nevertheless, as a developing region, this spread of countries have exhibited quite dramatic rates of growth. In 1962, for example, South Korea was ranked 99th in the world by GDP, along with the Sudan and Zaire, two of the world's poorest nations. By 1999 it was ranked 46th, having moved up more than 50 places. During the 1980s it grew at a spectacular average of 9,4 per cent annually, and during the 1990s at an average of 5,7 per cent (Cohen 2000; *The Economist* 2002).

Unlike its American counterpart in Latin America, Japanese influence in East Asian development has been overwhelmingly beneficial.

Conclusion

You may have noticed some curious things in our discussion of regulation theory and post-Fordism. First, regulation theory takes factors of government and politics much more seriously than many other neo-Marxist theories. This is, after all, what regulation refers to, the role of government and of consumer values in shaping economic accumulation. That is a significant move away from economic determinism.

Secondly, the contribution of post-Fordism in the Japanese flying geese policy has been very positive for countries in the region. That, again, is quite contrary to the development pessimism shown by other neo-Marxist theories. This is hardly a case of active underdevelopment! In short, regulation theory is in two respects a significant improvement over other neo-Marxist theories.

If, however, we look further back at all the neo-Marxist theories, there is another interesting aspect to note. Neo-Marxism introduced into development studies the notion of development within a global system. However, they have each worked with quite different ideas of how it operates. Imperialism theories saw capitalism duplicating itself in Third World countries after a period of destruction. Dependency, world system, and NIDL theories, for their part, saw core and peripheral countries as shaped by each other, but in a parasitic way. The core purposefully blocked development in the periphery. In regulation theory, much as in imperialism theories, capitalism duplicated itself where governments got their economic policies right. And finally, under post-Fordism, in East Asia, theorists saw a system, but a beneficial, not a parasitic, one.

By way of concluding this section, note also that in our consideration of neo-Marxist theories we have moved from an analysis which placed great emphasis on unequal relations of trade to one which focuses on systems of production. We have likewise seen a shift from an emphasis on economic factors to one which includes political and cultural factors also. All of these are important advances in the sophistication of Marxist theory.

In the next chapter we pursue this latter version of globalization in more detail through exploring the writing of Manuel Castells.

4 Castells: Informational Capitalism

For Manuel Castells there is a new modern global order based on what he calls 'informational capitalism'. This differs from previous eras in social, political, economic, and cultural ways.

Introduction

In this section we progress to the work of Manuel Castells, whose work entitled *The Information Age: Economy, Society and Culture* (2000), written in three volumes, provides a comprehensive and entertaining perspective on the contemporary global order. In considering Marxist and neo-Marxist approaches to globalization and development we started by discussing first dependency theory and world system theory. Secondly, we moved to NIDL theory, and then thirdly to the rise of the East Asian economies. Finally, Castells' insights into 'the network society' take us one step further into a more recent, and a more comprehensive, view of the global order. We shall see that it entails a different form of production (the informational economy), a different organization of corporations (via networking), a different notion of culture (the culture of virtual reality) and identity, a specific view on politics (the collapse of the state), and the prospect of total exclusion for some regions in the world ('black holes'). It is also important that Castells combines an economic perspective with both a political and a cultural/identity one – responding in an important way to the ongoing critique of neo-Marxist literature.

In the following discussion we will examine three broad aspects of Castells' view:
* the cultural;
* the political, and
* the economic.

Each of these aspects has both a broad macro-structural impact on the Third World, and a more detailed, quite personal, micro-sociological impact. Many of these aspects you will have experienced yourself. This discussion will not cover all of Castells' massive work, but it will give us an important slice of it which is relevant to development.

The culture of real virtuality

For Castells, real virtuality depicts a situation in which the real world and the media image have become so intertwined that they are difficult to tell apart. It is a situation where everyday life has become so soaked in media-generated symbols that one continually runs into the other, and the boundaries between the two have become blurred. Consider Castells' example. In the American presidential campaign of 1992 the vice-president, Dan Quayle, took exception to the actions of a character in a television programme, entitled *Murphy Brown*. In this programme a fictional woman called Murphy Brown, played by a real actress, Candice Bergen, decided to have a baby without being married. For Quayle this was an undermining of the integrity of the American family, and he said as much in a public speech on television. The response to this critique came, not from the actress, Candice Bergen, but from the character Murphy Brown. In an ensuing episode of the programme Dan Quayle was shown making his televised speech, and Murphy Brown defended her actions in the name of women's rights. The intriguing aspect of this event is that Dan Quayle was in dialogue with a television character, not a real person. Reality and the television image had become entangled and blurred (Castells 2000 (vol 1): 405).

Another example of this phenomenon is theme parks and the various Disneyworlds. Here fictional characters and situations are presented as real. One can shake the hand of Mickey Mouse and Donald Duck. One can sail down an underground river which travels through the world of Peter Pan, Captain Hook, and Tinkerbell. One can sit in a boat while the monster shark, Jaws, circles the boat and eventually attacks. Here fictional characters take on real and concrete existence. The principle of the real/virtual 'theme' has spread to shops and to shopping malls, and to waterfront areas.

What is important also is that more and more kinds of communication are incorporated into the electronic medium, so that, in some parts of the world, very little happens outside of the medium any more – not religion, nor learning, nor politics, not shopping, not banking, nor personal communication. Teenagers, who spend on average four hours a day watching television, then sit at a computer or pick up a cell-phone to convey their thoughts, about those television programmes, to their friends. Their lives are almost completely enclosed in a media-dominated world.

> Castells' picture of the world is a complex and multifaceted one that includes economic, political, cultural, criminal, and financial aspects.

There was a time, says Castells, when human society was dominated by nature. This was followed by a period in which humans dominated nature. We have now reached a third stage where society is gradually breaking free from nature altogether, floating off on its own into a different dimension. Human beings have created a completely new world woven out of their imaginations. What remains of nature is itself reconstructed in consumer forms as heritage sites, museums, and nature conservation or wilderness areas (Castells 2000 (vol 1): 508). Of course, what remains of the wilderness in wilderness sites has been reshaped, commoditized, and incorporated into a global tourism context.

Globalization and identity

It is a central characteristic of the Internet/television age that individuals are flooded with information. The variety of possible scenarios, cultures, value systems, styles, approaches, languages, is staggering. And they are presented in beguiling and seductive ways. Buddhist religion, Japanese martial arts, Indian kamasutra, to name but three, have all spread across the world.

Under these conditions traditional beliefs come under threat. It becomes extremely difficult to defend a belief on the grounds that it is the sole and absolute truth, that there are no competing truths. For every tradition, custom

In the first book of this series, *What is Sociology?* (page 4), relativizing is discussed as part of the sociological imagination, a process whereby social practices are put into comparative perspective across cultures and historical time.

and historically transmitted value, it now seems, there are dozens of others. One of the prime influences of globalization is that it *relativizes* beliefs, values, religions, traditions, customs. Traditions can no longer be justified on the basis that they are unique, or that they have existed since 'time immemorial', or that they are divinely ordained.

It is clear, then, that globalization poses a profound threat to the way certain belief systems justify themselves. There are two ways to respond to this threat. One is to construct different ways of establishing values, to find different values on which to justify decisions.

Another is to re-impose the old ways with greater force. That is the origin of fundamentalism – a forceful insistence that traditions can only be justified by resorting to holy texts. These different responses are at the root, says Castells, of the significant rise in the late twentieth century of cultural nationalism, of territorial communes and of religious fundamentalism. They are all forms of resistance to globalization.

> When the world becomes too large to be controlled, social actors aim at shrinking it back to their size and reach. When networks dissolve time and space, people anchor themselves in places, and recall their historic memory. When the patriarchal sustainment of personality breaks down, people affirm the transcendent value of family and community, as God's will (Castells 2000 (vol 1): 66).

These social forms are not confined to any one part of the world. They appear in both First World and Third World countries. Examples are the Taliban of Afghanistan, the Zapatistas of Mexico, the American militia of the United States, the Aum Shinrikyo of Japan. However, when they appear in the Third World, they often appear in the context of extreme poverty and desperation. That can have ominous consequences, as we shall see.

The crisis of the state

We shall see further on that the network society has the capacity to connect highly specialized personnel and flexible organizations across the globe. They are drawn into nodes of intense and highly profitable activity. On the other hand, the same network excludes significant sections of the world's population. At times these are groups or regions within relatively wealthy countries, such as the homeless and illiterate ghettoes of urban America. At other times it is whole countries which drop out of the loop of the global economy. For our purposes it is the latter example which concerns us, because large parts of Africa have, says Castells, fallen into this black hole. They are trapped in a structural position from which it is extremely difficult to escape. They are no longer even part of the Third World, they have become, he says, the Fourth World.

Partly this is a technological phenomenon. Places which have no electricity, no telephones, minimal education, simply cannot connect. They cannot be part of the Internet economy. It has no use for them. Partly also this is a political phenomenon, and it relates to the collapse of the state as a national institution. Global currents put national governments under enormous pressure. They are called upon to deal with problems that are beyond their capacity. For example, no country can on its own hope to combat international drug trafficking. It is forced into alliance with other countries, with international anti-crime organizations. Much the same applies in the spheres of global finance, environmental pollution, political terrorism, global warming, to name but a few. States are simply too small to deal with these problems effectively.

At the same time we have seen that one of the ways in which people resist the threats to their beliefs and identities is to resort to local communes, to regional organization, to smaller more manageable organizational forms. To repeat, 'When the world becomes too large to be controlled, social actors aim at shrinking it back to their size and reach'.

What this means is that the national state is being sandwiched between bigger global organizations and smaller local organizations. 'National governments in the Information Age are too small to handle global forces, yet too big to manage people's lives' (Castells 2000).

Another aspect of the crisis of the state as an institution, and a chilling one for Africa, is the criminalization of the state. This refers to the way in which some African leaders (and they are not the only political leaders in the world who have done this) have used their positions as leaders to enrich themselves to a huge degree. They have become parasites on their own societies. The most infamous case in this regard is Zaire's Mobutu Sese Seko. Within the context of the Cold War he benefited immensely from Western backing – to the tune of US$10 billion by 1993:

> *For three decades, he put his vast country, the second largest in sub-Saharan Africa at the disposal of the CIA and other Western agencies, which used it as a staging base for their activities throughout the continent. In exchange, he enjoyed a free hand at home, diverting for his use billions of dollars from Zaire's mineral wealth while leaving most Zaireans in poverty* (quoted from Kempster in Castells 2000 (vol 3): 99).

While Mobutu is the best known, he is by no means the only example. Others include Sani Abacha of Nigeria, Félix Houphouet-Boigny of Ivory Coast, and Jean-Bedel Bokassa of the Central African Republic.

International crime

Countries of the Fourth World can be an extreme danger to global stability and development.

The circle of Castells' global dynamic closes when, first, we take the exclusion of countries and regions from the information economy, secondly, the crisis of the state as an institution, and thirdly, the African 'predatory' state, and these we now add the global criminal economy (see figure 4.1 below).

International criminal organizations are nothing new. But new forms of communication and new opportunities for moving finances have expanded the scope for global crime. Estimates on the extent of such activity vary between US$500 billion to US$1 trillion in the year of 1994 (Castells 2000 (vol 3): 172). Criminal activities include not only drug trafficking, which is the biggest source of income, but also trafficking in weapons, nuclear material, illegal immigrants, women and children, and finally money laundering. Criminal groups include the Sicilian mafia, the American mafia, Colombian cartels, Mexican cartels, Nigerian networks, the Chinese triads, the Japanese *yakuza*, the Russian *mafiyas*, and the Jamaican *posses* (Castells 2000 (vol 3): 170).

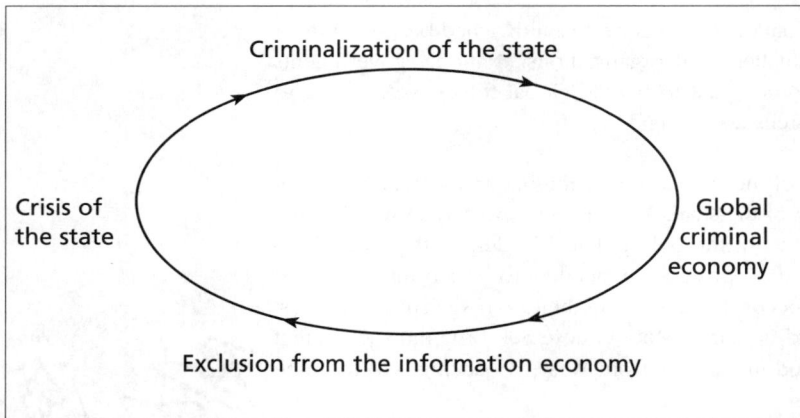

Criminalization of the state

Crisis of the state

Global criminal economy

Exclusion from the information economy

Fig 4.1: Factors in global poverty

We do not need to follow Castells into all the details of the activities of organized crime. For our purposes, two consequences can be highlighted. One is the further undermining of the political process and of government capacity by the buying of political influence by organized crime. In many countries of the world politicians are substantially under the influence of criminal networks.

The second is the use by organized crime of precisely those areas of the world which have been excluded from the new economy. In these areas money laundering and a wide range of trafficking profit from the lack of security, and law and order. The trade in women, children, and immigrants is also frequently sourced from these areas. In other words, it is precisely those areas which have been excluded from the informational economy, where populations are caught in an inescapable trap of poverty and desperation, that organized crime finds fruitful for its various purposes.

The picture Castells sketches as a possible future global scenario is a frightening one. It combines black holes of development with the collapsing state, with organized crime, with fundamentalism – drawn into a self-strengthning downward spiral. Remember that this was written long before the 11 September 2001 attack on the World Trade Centre in New York:

> *The dream of a shrunk planet made out of a highly productive, very affluent, avid consumer minority, floating on a cloud over low-skill generic labor, and ignoring the black holes to where devalued people and locales are doomed, it is simply an untenable nightmare, inhabited by fundamentalist reactions, and desperate terrorist threats* (Castells 1998: 9).

The new economy: ICT and finance

At the heart of the new global economy, says Castells, are, first, information and communications technology (ICT) and, secondly finance. The ICT sector has itself provided for massive increases in employment, financial investment, and stock market activity. (We all know what happened eventually to the 'dot.com bubble'. In 2001 it collapsed.) As a new engine of economic growth it paralleled the earlier technological revolutions that flowed from steam, electricity, and the internal combustion engine (that is, motor cars).

More importantly, however, information technology has gradually spread into other sectors of the economy, transforming these and raising productivity quite significantly. The world economic boom of the 1990s was largely driven by the ICT sector, by the technological innovation which came with it, and the staggering amounts of money people were prepared to invest in it.

At the same time as informational technology was transforming productivity activity, it also helped to transform the financial sector. During the late 1980s and the 1990s not only did financial activity become possible through the touch of a computer button, but the obstacles to cross-border financial flows were removed. Within a brief period of time billions of dollars worth of shares, bonds, currencies, and other financial instruments were being traded around the world. In currencies alone trade was worth US$1,5 trillion in 1998.

This was extremely dangerous for Third World countries, and even for some First World countries. It meant that the money of a particular country could be bought and sold like any other commodity. More critically, the price of that currency was now at the mercy of supply and demand, and of speculation. The price of the South African rand (2001), the Argentinian peso (2002), the

Thai baht (1997), the Malaysian ringgit (1998), could and did fluctuate wildly at particular times. Such wild movements wreaked havoc with economies and with societies. Thousands of people lost their jobs. Companies went bankrupt. National governments themselves could go bankrupt and be unable to act to save their economies.

What is new about this new global system is that it is able to operate 'as a unit in real time'. What that means is that transactions can cross the globe almost instantaneously. People thousands of kilometres apart can work together as if they were standing next to one another and talking.

This new capacity has given birth to a new form of organization, the network enterprise. This is an enterprise which works through networking, continually combining and recombining various companies and parts of companies in ever-changing and temporary patterns, depending solely on the project that needs to be carried out. Once a project has been completed that particular network dissolves and the elements of it recombine around another project. In some cases this development has favoured small and medium-size enterprises over the very large. The very large, where they have continued, have needed to reorganize themselves on new principles, so that their smaller parts can participate in this process of combining and recombining.

One of the consequences of this new organization is the fragmentation and weakening of labour. While the network enterprise combines and integrates management, expertise and planning across the globe, it makes organization and protection by the unions ever more difficult:

> *The extraordinary increase in flexibility and adaptability permitted by new technologies opposed the rigidity of labor to the mobility of capital. ... Productivity and profitability were enhanced, yet labor lost institutional protection and became increasingly dependent on individual bargaining conditions in a constantly changing labor market* (Castells 2000 (vol 1): 302).

All of this was driven under the umbrella of neo-liberal ideology, and led by Ronald Reagan of the United States, Margaret Thatcher of Great Britain, and Helmut Kohl of Germany.

Where does Castells go wrong?

The first thing to notice about Castells' writing about the information society is that it is difficult to pin down. Castells is an enormously eclectic writer. He draws on a very wide range of authors and theories; he covers economic, political, cultural, and managerial aspects with equal ease. All of that is good, and a great improvement on the earlier neo-Marxist theories we discussed.

But he does very little to consolidate his own position. If one were to ask where Castells fits, what his theoretical position is, it would not be easy to give a clear answer. Is that a problem? Surely, so the postmodernists would argue, the world we live in is an enormously varied and fragmented reality. Theories should reflect that.

That is true, but we need to be more specific than that. It is true that the world Castells describes is not the whole world. What he concentrates on is a node of high energy, mobility and profitability which is at the epicentre of this strange new world. He is quite clear that not everyone is part of this epicentre.

However, at the same time, it is an epicentre of enormous power and of truly global dimensions. It has the capacity to destroy whole countries, for example, in the speed of its currency movements. And it does not matter where those countries are. No country or economy is safe from that predatory effect. There is something quite murderously uniform, unfragmented, and un-eclectic about that effect. Being postmodern about that is like saying that a tidal wave is made up of very loose and uncoordinated bits. There is something contradictory about that.

Conclusion

In this chapter we have seen how Manuel Castells combines economic and cultural perspectives to paint a picture of a globally organized world with very particular features and important consequences for development. The features of this new world are:

- The culture of real virtuality, a culture in which reality and fiction become more and more confused.
- A world progressively enclosed in media, in which 'nature' has become a reconstructed product for sale.
- A much weakened state institution unable to perform the roles it has traditionally done, and vulnerable to corruption.
- The spread of organized crime and religious fundamentalism, both of which make use of developmental 'black holes' to more conveniently further their activities.
- An informational economy driven by information and communications technology, and producing a new form of corporate organization, the network enterprise.

The implications for development are frightening. It means that certain parts of the world which have neither the technology nor the skills to participate in these high value activities are simply excluded. They become the Fourth World, left behind by the march of capitalist development, but striking back at the First World through terror, through conflict, through migration, through disease. It is not a situation that we can afford to ignore.

Epilogue

At the beginning of this book (page 1) I set down as an important principle that I would be pursuing four continuing themes throughout this book. These were:

- The economic development of the East Asian tigers.
- The improving sophistication of neo-Marxist theories.
- The way in which globalization has been thought through by various theories.
- The conversation which has gone on between theories.

We do not have the space to summarize the various steps along the way in each of the those four. Here I will simply point out some of the interesting lines of thought one might follow with regard to globalization. Consider the figure below.

Fig: Views on globalization

Theory	Views on globalization	Implications for development
Modernization	Largely ignored	Optimistic
Dependency	Core versus periphery	Very pessimistic
World system	Core, semi-periphery, periphery	Not quite so pessimistic
NIDL	MNCs in development enclaves	Less pessimistic
Regulation	Distorted Fordism	Mildly optimistic
Post-Fordism	Regional cooperation with Japan as leader	Very optimistic
Castells	Self-confirming cycle of politics, technology, culture, financial speculation	Very pessimistic for Africa

Modernization theory, particularly its earlier sociological variant, simply ignored globalization by pretending, for example, that colonialism was either not important or was beneficial to Third World development. Dependency theory criticized modernization theory precisely for this stunning gap.

Theories of imperialism introduced the notion that capitalism was a necessarily transnational, and eventually, global phenomenon, but they did not understand the systemic nature of this expansion. These writers thought that capitalism would eventually duplicate itself in Third World countries.

Dependency theory was the first truly global systems theory of capitalist development. It divided the world into core and peripheral parts, each shaped by the influence of the other. Immanuel Wallerstein's world system theory pushed this concept further by dividing the world into three layers, instead of two. For both Frank and Wallerstein development, if it was going to happen at all, would have to happen within the framework of an exploitative and unequal global framework.

NIDL theory took that same concept and shifted it slightly by showing that certain peripheral countries now hosted important manufacturing activities. This was development, but it was flawed enclave development.

Regulation theory was a strange response within this context. Because it almost abandoned a global framework altogether, working almost with a neo-liberal notion of countries competing in an open world market. It proposed that Third World economies were of minimal importance to the First World.

Post-Fordist studies of East Asia returned to the global idea, but turned it around by seeing it as benevolent and fruitful for the East Asian region rather than inhibiting. East Asian countries within the Japanese sphere of influence had benefited substantially by their regional integration.

Castells, finally, builds a more complex and multifaceted notion of globalization, with political, cultural, economic, technological, and criminal elements to it. This global system generates periodic waves of currency speculation which are disastrous for Third World countries. It also produces Fourth World black holes in which regions of the world, such as Africa, are completely cut off from investment.

Exercises

It has been an important concern of this book to present development material in a way that constitutes a number of ongoing themes. The exercises here continue that concern for coherent argument. Social science is not about the recitation of hundreds of facts and figures. It is much more about the way that this material is ordered, argued, criticized, and mobilized. And, if it were necessary, there is a great deal of educational theory to support that approach (Ramsden 1992). The exercises suggested below, then, work from the simpler to the more challenging.

The exercises below come in different forms, some easier and some more difficult. The easier ones (let's call them **Level A** questions) typically ask you to do things such as:
- 'define' concepts;
- 'explain what' writer X says about something, or
- 'summarize' what writer Y says about something else.

This is relatively easy because it asks you simply to understand what a writer is saying and to express it in your own words.

Slightly more difficult questions (**Level B questions) ask you to:**
- 'explain how' A links with B according to Marx or Parsons;
- 'compare and contrast' modernization theory and dependency theory, or
- 'apply' modernization theory in a particular situation.

These questions take some extra thought because you are being asked to transpose ideas from one situation to another.

You may also be asked to:
- 'construct a careful argument about …'. In this case you are required to put together a coherent story which has logical and reasoned steps which follow from one another.

The most difficult, and the most interesting, questions (**Level C**) ask you to:
- 'construct your own examples of' a particular concept;
- 'discuss/critically evaluate' the ideas of, or the argument of, theory A, or
- 'do you agree with' this or that view.

These are again more difficult because you have to start being creative and mobilize your own independent thoughts. They will also be somewhat longer questions because you will require further space to mobilize the steps of your argument. In the assessment of academic work, this skill is also considered the most valuable one.

Let us now consider some concrete examples from the material of this book.

Exercises

Level A
Give brief definitions of the following terms, and where appropriate indicate which theory they belong to:
- relative deprivation;
- absolute poverty;
- per capita GNP;
- evolutionary universals;
- value consensus;
- EPZ;
- enclave development;
- structural adjustment programme;
- Keynesian policies, and
- neo-liberal policies.

Level B
Explain how:
1. a global perspective undermines evolutionist notions of historical change.
2. dependency theory sees the relationship between core and periphery.
3. world system theory sees the possibility of (dependent) development.
4. NIDL theory understands the super-exploitation of women.
5. some countries of the world fall into a 'black hole' according to Castells.

Compare and contrast:
6. how dependency theory and world system theory see the prospects for development in peripheral countries.
7. how Fordism and post-Fordism think about the organization of labour.
8. how neo-liberalism and Keynesianism consider the role of the state in development.

Level C
Do you agree with:
9. Castells' view that informational capitalism has significantly contributed to fundamentalist terrorism and global crime? Give reasons.
10. the Keynesian view that states must intervene actively and purposefully in Third World economies? Give reasons.

Longer essay questions

11 Globalization sees the world as operating as a single system with significant influence over all its parts. Give a critical discussion of how various development theories have either ignored, or made use of, the concept of globalization. (You could use the table and the discussion in the Epilogue to get your essay going.)

12 One of the key criticisms of neo-Marxist theories has been that they have been excessively economistic. Give a critical discussion of this assertion, using examples from the various theories mentioned in this book.

13 Evaluate the way in which various neo-Marxist theories have explained the remarkable economic development during the 1980s and 1990s of the East Asian tigers and dragons.

Annotated Bibliography

Cohen, R, & P Kennedy (2000) *Global Sociology* London: Macmillan Press.
   Written as a textbook for students, this book offers an excellent and easily accessible overview of the field of globalization.

Haralambos, M, & M Holborn (2000) *Sociology: Themes and Perspectives*, 6th edition, London: Collins Educational.
   One of the most thorough textbooks available today for sociology students. It deals with an extremely wide range of relevant topics.

May, J (ed) (2000) *Poverty and Inequality in South Africa: Meeting the Challenge* Cape Town & New York: David Philip & Zed Books.
   A detailed and thorough treatment of poverty in South Africa today. Quite technical in parts, but it is the most up-to-date discussion of the subject.

Todaro, M (2000) *Economic Development*, 7th edition, Harlow: Addison Welsey Longman.
   Also a textbook, but written for economics students. It covers a number of important areas relevant to our discussion. Well worth pursuing.

Webster, A (1990) *Introduction to the Sociology of Development*, 2nd edition, London: Macmillan Press.
   A brief but solid introduction to theoretical aspects of development.

Wilson, F, & M Ramphele (1989) *Uprooting Poverty: The South African Challenge* Cape Town: David Philip.
   This is the book that pulled together the voluminous 1984 Second Carnegie Inquiry into Poverty in Southern Africa. An excellent treatment of the issue.

Bibliography

Aglietta, M (1979) *A Theory of Capitalist Regulation: The US Experience* London: New Left Books.

Castells, M (1996) *The Information Age: Economy, Society and Culture*, Volume 1: *The Rise of the Network Society* Oxford: Blackwell.

— (2000) *End of Millennium* Oxford: Blackwell.

Coetzee, J, J Graaff, F Hendricks, & G Wood (eds) (2001) *Development: Theory, Policy, and Practice* Cape Town: Oxford University Press.

Cohen, R, & P Kennedy (2000) *Global Sociology* London: Macmillan Press.

Darwin, C (1968) *On the Origin of Species* Harmondsworth: Penguin.

The Economist (2002) *Pocket World in Figures* London: Profile Books.

Foster-Carter, A (1978) 'The modes of production controversy' *New Left Review* 107.

Frank, AG (1967) *Capitalism and Underdevelopment in Latin America* New York: Monthly Review.

Fröbel, V et al (1980) *The New International Division of Labour* Cambridge: Cambridge University Press.

Gelb, S (1991) 'South Africa's economic crisis: an overview' *South Africa's Economic Crisis* Cape Town: David Philip.

Gereffi, G (1994) 'Capitalism, development and global commodity chains' in L Sklair *Capitalism and Development* London and New York: Routledge.

Giddens, A (1984) *The Constitution of Society* Cambridge: Cambridge University Press.

Graaff, J (2001) *What is Sociology?* Cape Town: Oxford University Press.

Hallpike, CR (1986) *The Principles of Social Evolution* Oxford: Clarendon Press.

Haralambos, M, & M Holborn (1995) *Sociology: Themes and Perspectives*, 6th edition, London: Collins Educational.

Hill, RYL (1994) 'Japanese Multinationals and East Asian development: the case of the Automobile Industry' in L Sklair *Capitalism and Development* London and New York: Routledge.

Horwitz, R (1967) *The Political Economy of South Africa* London: Weidenfeld & Nicholson.

Innes, D (1984) *Anglo: Anglo American and the Rise of South Africa* Johannesburg: Ravan Press.

Lenin, VI (1966) *Imperialism: The Highest Stage of Capitalism* Moscow: Progress Publishers.

Lipietz, A (1987) *Mirages and Miracles: The Crisis of Global Fordism* London: New Left Books.

Lipton, M (1985) *Capitalism and Apartheid: South Africa 1910–1986* Aldershot: Wildwood House.

Marais, H (2001) *South Africa: Limits to Change: The Political Economy of Transition* Cape Town: Zed Books and UCT Press.

Marx, K (1976) *Capital*, Volume 1, Harmondsworth: Penguin.

May, J (ed) (2000) *Poverty and Inequality in South Africa: Meeting the Challenge* Cape Town & New York: David Philip & Zed Books.

Mittelman, J (1995) 'Rethinking the international division of labour in the context of globalization' *Third World Quarterly* 16 (2): 273–95.

O'Dowd, M (1997) *The O'Dowd Thesis and the Triumph of Democratic Liberalism* Sandton: The Free Market Foundation.

Parsons, T (1966) *The Evolution of Societies* Englewood Cliffs: Prentice Hall.

Preston, PW (1996) *Development Theory: An Introduction* Oxford: Blackwell.

Ramsden, P (1992) *Learning to Teach in Higher Education* London: Routledge/ Farmer.

Rostow, W (1960) *The Stages of Economic Growth: A Non-Communist Manifesto* Cambridge, Cambridge University Press.

Sklair, L (1994) *Capitalism and Development* London: Routledge.

So, A (1990) *Social Change and Development* London: Sage.

Taylor, V (2000) *South Africa: Transformation for Human Development* Pretoria: UNDP.

Todaro, M (2000) *Economic Development*, 7th edition, Harlow: Addison Welsey Longman.

Wallerstein, I (1974) *The Modern World System*, Volume I: *Capitalist Agriculture and the Origins of the European World-economy in the Sixteenth Century* New York: Academic Press.

—— (1980) *The Modern World System*, Volume II: *Mercantilism and the Consolidation of the European World-economy, 1600–1750* New York: Academic Press.

—— (1988) *The Modern World System*, Volume III: *The Second Era of Great Expansion of the Capitalist World-economy, 1730–1840* New York: Academic Press.

Webster, A (1990) *Introduction to the Sociology of Development*, 2nd edition, London: Macmillan Press.

Wilson, F, & M Ramphele (1989) *Uprooting Poverty: The South African Challenge* Cape Town: David Philip.

Wolpe, H (1972) 'Capitalism and cheap labour power in South Africa' *Economy and Society* 1: 426–56.

Wright, E, A Levine, & E Sober (1992) *Reconstructing Marxism* London: Verso.

Glossary

Absolute poverty: the condition of people who are unable to provide for their most basic physical survival needs

Capitalism: an economic and political system in which a country's trade and industry are controlled by private owners for profit, rather than by the state

Culture of real virtuality: a way of living in which media and other realities become indistinguishable

Dependency theory: propagated by André Gunder Frank, explains Third World underdevelopment through the active underdevelopment of peripheral countries by core countries

Dragons: East Asian economies which have grown extremely rapidly over the last two decades – Indonesia, Malaysia, Philippines, Thailand

Economic determinism: a view of society in which economic forces are seen as the most important determinants of the form a society takes

Enclave development: in dependency, world system and NIDL theories, development in Third World countries which is enclosed in a small area and has minimal impact on the broader economy of that country

Evolutionary universals: in Parsonian theory, those elements in societies which are necessary for historical development to progress

Evolutionism: a theory of history which sees social change as gradual, progressive, irreversible, repeatable, converging to a single societal type, and predictable

Fordism: a form of production initiated by Henry Ford based on conveyor-belt mass production and tight supervision of labour

Functionalism: a form of argument which proposes that parts have beneficial roles (functions) for the whole

Gross national product (GNP): the total value of all the goods and services produced in a country in a particular year

Household Subsistence Level (HSL): the amount of money that is necessary to provide a household (of six people) with the very elementary necessities to stay alive; those basic necessities include food, clothing, fuel or lighting, washing, rent, and transport

Human Development Index (HDI): a broader measure of development designed by the UNDP which includes income, life expectancy, and educational attainment

Imperialism: a policy of extending a country's power and influence through colonization or other means

Informational capitalism: a form of economic activity which relies substantially on the sale and purchase of skills related to knowledge and information

Keynesianism: macro-economic theory which proposes state intervention in the market in order to stimulate growth and provide welfare services for poorer people

Merchant capitalism: an early form of capitalism based on trade, and particularly on the slave trade

68

Minimum Economic Level (MEL): the MLL multiplied one and a half times

Minimum Living Level (MLL): the amount of money that is necessary to provide an individual or a household (of six people) with the very elementary necessities to stay alive; those basic necessities include food, clothing, fuel or lighting, washing, rent, and transport

Modernity: the condition of First World societies in the nineteenth, twentieth, and twenty-first centuries, often refers to cultural, intellectual, and scientific aspects

Modernization: the process of achieving modernity

Modernization theory: explains Third World lack of development mainly through cultural backlogs, the so-called 'shackles of tradition'

Neo-liberalism: macro-economic theory based on free market principles, propagated initially by Margaret Thatcher and Ronald Reagan

Neo-Marxists: in contrast to orthodox Marxists, explain Third World underdevelopment through mechanisms of unequal trade

New international division of labour theory (NIDL): propagated by Volker Fröbel and associates, explains Third World dependent development through the transfer of industrial production to Third World countries

Orthodox Marxists: contrary to neo-Marxists, explain Third World underdevelopment through the exploitation of labour

Pattern variables: in Parsonian theory, the attributes of, respectively, primitive and modern forms of social interaction

Post-Fordism: contrary to Fordism, a form of production initiated by Toyota Motor Corporation based on flexible machinery and labour

Regulation theory: explains capitalist development through the interaction of regimes of accumulation (production), modes of regulation (economic policy), and consumer preferences

Relative deprivation: the experience of poverty which is influenced by society's expectations and values

Structural poverty: situation of people whose advancement is blocked by patterns of power and discrimination in society

Theories of imperialism: explain economic development as the result of capitalism's drive to go outside of national boundaries

Tigers: East Asian economies which have grown exceptionally fast in the last two decades – South Korea, Taiwan, Singapore, Hong Kong

World system theory: propagated by Immanuel Wallerstein, explains Third World underdevelopment through unequal trade and political relationships between core, semi-peripheral, and peripheral countries

Index